PRAISE FOR J.R. SOLONCHE

[His] work is varied in its aims and form (the ghazals, sonnets, and anaphora poems stand out), though united by a pithy, sardonic voice that can achieve playfulness, profundity, and mystery in the same breath. I admire their fearlessness and honesty.

— Joshua Coben

Many times, poets with as many books under their belt as Solonche tend to assume a sage-like persona, presenting themselves as the wise old bard who has the answer to your every question about the universe—including that murkiest thought in the hindquarters of your brain—tucked conveniently up their sleeves. You can practically feel their feet lifting off of the ground as they imagine themselves hovering just a few inches above the rest of man and womankind. The glory of J.R. Solonche is that, over the course of his career (read: over the course of his *life*) he has been consistently able to keep his feet firmly on the ground.He achieves this through humor. He achieves this through quirkiness. He achieves this through self-deprecation. And sometimes he achieves this through a combination of the three.

— Stephen Cramer is the winner of the National Poetry Series and the Louise Bogan Award

According to Lord Polonius in *Hamlet*, "brevity is the soul of wit." In the poetry of J. R. Solonche, brevity, soul and wit co-exist superbly. Start with any of his poems. You'll find, unlike much of what is written these days, the wit is never far from the surface. As for the brevity, imagine an appetizer that's as filling as a main course. And, after the meal, after the laughter, the soul will be what lingers.

— John Grey, author of *What Else Is There,* Main Street Rag's Editor's Poetry Series

Solonche, an accomplished poet, employs various forms in this compilation, including haiku, prose poem, and free verse. The poems often imaginatively enter into the natural or material world via anthropomorphic similes... Many works have an aphoristic quality that recall Zen koans, and they can be playfully amusing or even silly... A strong set of sympathetic but never sentimental observations.

— *Kirkus Reviews*

The spirit of Horace, the melancholy of time slithering away and turning all to dust, tempered with art, wit, and good grace.

— Ricardo Nirenberg, editor of *Offcourse: A Literary Journal*

J.R.Solonche's many books of poetry, one nominated for a Pulitzer Prize, reveal a wry and vivid wit, a sharp but sympathetic eye, and a respect for the homely but significant detail, all wedded to an acute social and cultural consciousness. In his imaginative progress through city streets and country roads, the commonplace becomes the extraordinary... In lines full of mischief or romance, gaiety or grief, he is the poet of the every day, spent on earth or in an imaginary heaven.

— Judith Farr, author of *What Lies Beyond: Poems* and *The Passion of Emily Dickinson*

The best feature of Solonche's poetry is its diversity. Everyone who encounters this volume (including the postman who delivers it to you) will find something in it to understand and remember — and a great deal to enjoy.

— Tony Beyer is author of *Anchor Stone*, finalist for the New Zealand Book Award.

The history of book blurbs is littered with high falutin' praise, whacky and wild metaphors, written to impress not to inform. All I need to say about J.R. Solonche's poems is that they are good, really, really good. So much so that they have a high "I-wish-I'd-written-that" factor. That's a compliment I hand out to very few poets writing today. You want wit? You want humor? You want erudition? You want them all mixed into poems? Try Solonche. You won't be disappointed. Envious perhaps, but not disappointed.

— John Murphy is editor of *The Lake Contemporary Poetry Webzine.*

The tone is established from the outset: wry, wise, sardonic and playful, drawing the reader irresistibly in. Solonche is revealed as a philosopher in the mould of Wittgenstein: aphoristic, charismatic, acerbic and oddly mystical. If you met this book in a bar, you would definitely want to take it home with you and every day thereafter congratulate yourself on how lucky you've been. But that is true of all his books.

— David Mark Williams

Abandon all bullshit ye who enter here. J. R. Solonche's new collection is *Enjoy Yourself,* and he means it. Here is where the questions lead not to a comforting mystery but to the courage needed to live not *with* the questions but with no answers. Look into the abyss with Solonche and be amazed at all he doesn't see. As he declares in the poem "Testimony," "I want to prove a poet can do this without telling it slant." Lest you are thinking, "Oh no, not another poet savoring his despair," know that in poem after poem you will welcome a wry smile. And in the end, after all the bullshit has been has been cleared away, enters his daughter evoking his love and a father's sigh, and the anything but slant yet nuanced assurance that "And now, when they ask me, I will answer,/with passion of my own, and with my own/audacious authority. *Go out and listen to the moon./It speaks for you.*

— Jack Ridl is the author of *Saint Peter and the Goldfinch,* and *Practicing to Walk Like a Heron,* named best collection of poetry by ForeWord/Indie Press Review

These short poems are an extraordinary amalgam of wit, close observation, humor, and clear-seeing. Each one singles out and illuminates an ordinary moment – ordinary, that is, until the poet explodes into a miniature epiphany. Easy of access and frequently profound, J.R. Solonche's poems induce in me a state of delighted surprise.

— Chase Twichell is the author of Horses *Where the Answers Should Have Been: New and Selected Poems*

J.R. Solonche

Selected Poems

2002 - 2021

SERVING
HOUSE
BOOKS

Selected Poems: 2002-2021

Copyright © 2021 by J.R. Solonche

All Rights Reserved

Published by Serving House Books
Copenhagen, Denmark and South Orange, NJ
www.servinghousebooks.com

ISBN: 978-1-947175-51-8

Library of Congress Control Number: 2021934009

Member of The Independent Book Publishers Association

First Serving House Books Edition 2021

Author Photograph: Emily Solonche

Serving House Books Logo: Barry Lereng Wilmont

Contents

POETRY AS A PUBLIC MATTER

J.R. Solonche is truly an "American Poet." And what does this mean today, in 2021? We can look back at the significant turn in poetry-as-art with the "cultural revolution" — the 1960s — and notice how rock 'n roll broke meter into phrase and how truth was told directly, without artifice. I see this emblematically with Solonche's work, especially in this volume of poems selected from nearly 20 years of work. He keeps poetry's music but changes the tune with declarative, reportorial swing-songs. He addresses the everyday, chooses inspiration at the foot of Mt. Olympus where it's easier to breathe, talks to people and pigeons, and he's not afraid to say 'I love you' without adornment. It's a voice that could not have existed in the 1950s and it's an exemplary one for our time because this poet is about humanity, about you and me, with no fakery.

Selected Poems 2002 – 2021 shows us the breadth, with a fine brush, of J.R. Solonche -- a beloved poet. He is a minstrel with every tool crafted to accompany his voice. He's funny, he's sad, and he fits the moment. He's inventive, conversational, rhetorical, and mostly sounds like a member of the family. What makes this troubadour so engaging are his various poetic techniques. He writes in all forms, and the voice is inimitable each time. We might find him using anaphora's enchanting repetitions to keep a poem in play, as in "I Was Looking for the Important One." This poem is as political a statement as we need — to know that Big and Small are the same in this life, and certainly beyond:

> I was looking for the important one.
> I looked in the drawers.
> I looked in the closets.
> I looked in the pantry.
> I looked under the kitchen sink.
> I looked under the bathroom sink.
> I looked under the other bathroom sink.

I looked in the attic.
I looked in the basement.
I looked in the garage.
I looked on the book shelves.

....

I found it finally.
It was in the wastepaper basket.
It was under all the other important ones.

Even in this truncated version, we can enjoy the wit of a poet who confronts life's most profound questions with a clear and amused eye. This is the way I like to take my 'profundity,' and many other readers agree.

And the work of a poet is, after all, to ease us toward death, beautifully, or at least turn death around to fill it with as much life as possible. We look at "The Path" for this. There is such caring and compassion for the temporal appreciation of our world:

To know what will happen
never makes what happens easier.
The ash leaves seek one another
on the ground, to form again,

in the path's curve an ash tree,
and on the lawn of Morrison Hall
the brown and red leaves fall,
and in front of the library

maples get lost in light.
The faces blur into one face,
and the names, without a trace,
disappear overnight.

I see myself in the glass
of the door, a shadow, hurled
through the zero of the world.
Harmless, I pass

in, to disengage,
to read the maples lost
in light, to read the frost
coming on, to read a page

or two, to read the man
looking back in the glass
like a book I read once
and since have forgotten.

Each section in the book is a contour in Solonche's map during his writing years. Many poems are philosophical, many are obsessed with nature, and all are about the making and the meaning of poetry. In "Beauty," the poet takes an anecdote, a simple event, and turns it on its head:

From my room down the hall,
I can hear the mathematics
professor getting emotional
about an equation, and I ask
myself how someone can get
so worked up about what isn't real,
an abstraction, nothing but
signs and symbols. A scribble.

Oh, I say to myself. *To him
it is a poem, a formal one,
every word in place, every rhyme
perfect, every stanza exact. Poor man.
He, too, must pound the beauty in
with his fist. Every time. Every damn time.*

I believe this poet will be remembered for poetry that is vertical, slender, compressed to deliver tension and rigor. Here is "Time" in its entirety:

Neither yours to give
nor mine to take,
yet so warm
from our hands.

Please notice how the poet is always including the reader, never speaking from a catbird seat, never prophesying, always getting up close and natural, even when speaking of the most elusive and daunting subjects. This is called generosity. This is when we know the poet is one with his readers.

The absolute best remark I can make about this book is that I would give it to non-readers of poems as a conversion to poetry, for its language is as available as rain, hopeful as sunshine, and fresh as the wind. It's a perfect book to let the reading public know that this is America's poetry.

America

The notebook I am writing in was made in China.
The pen I am writing with was made in China.
The chair I am sitting on was made in China.
The desk I am sitting at was made in China.
The frames of the glasses I am seeing with were made
    in China.
The glass I am drinking from was made in China.
But the bourbon I am drinking was made in America.
And the poem I am writing was made in America.
And that's enough America for me.

This is a serious book disguised as playfulness, and we are its lucky recipients.

Grace Cavalieri, Maryland Poet Laureate

from *Peach Girl: Poems for a Chinese Daughter*   2002

BESIDE THE PEARL RIVER

Beside the Pearl River,
in a hotel with a waterfall

in the lobby, the White Swan,
my daughter sleeps between us

in a bed large enough for twenty daughters.
My heart is busy with many feelings,

but in my mind there are two thoughts
and then only one thought:

how the waterfall and the river
are like father and daughter:

how a father of one daughter is no less
a father than a father of twenty.

MY DAUGHTER SAYS GOODNIGHT

You say goodnight twenty
times and mean it, I suppose,
each time, and I say goodnight
twenty times in dutiful response
and each time mean it, I suppose,
and when, at the twentieth
goodnight, you go to sleep, it is
as if you are feigning sleep,
so quick the metamorphosis
from perpetual motion to no motion,
so sudden the collapse to the inert
shape beside me, armless, legless,
round at both ends, a burrower
half-buried in bed-burrow.
Even your breathing seems
faked as I turn over your form
from face-down animal
to two-legged, two-armed person,
a cadenced performance
measured to fool your captured
audience. Too young to fool me
because too young to fool yourself,
you wear no guilty glance or snaky grin.
Your face is calm to perfection.
The future takes shape there,
under cover of darkness.

DOING SEVENTY ON THE HIGHWAY

Doing seventy on the highway,
I look over at my wife. She is
sleeping. Her head is tilted
against the subtle curve of window.
In my mirrors, eighteen-wheelers
loom up out of nowhere, then spit
their headlights and pass, each
one a thunderstorm splitting
the horizon in front of me. White
thunderstorm. Red thunderstorm.
Yellow thunderstorm. I consider
doing seventy-five. I don't. Instead,
I look back at my daughter.
She is sleeping. Her head is dropped
on her chest. I reach behind and
push her chin up. Thus far this
summer this is summer's finest day.
The sky is blue pure through.
On the hood of my car, the sun
does a golden dance. Tell me,
Sol Invictus, what the speed
of darkness is. I have to go faster.

PRAYER

O god of daughters,
guard well this daughter,
guard well this daughter

with the thick-calloused
palm of your right hand,
guard well this daughter

with the power of your
male voice, loud as thunder,
profound as thunder

on the mountaintop,
guard well this daughter
with your broad expanse

of chest, resilient as the shield
of the stretched bull-hide,
guard well this daughter

with the sinews of your thighs
like the temple-columns
that carry the roof of the temple,

guard well this daughter
with the stern gaze of your eye,
ever-wakeful, ever-ablaze,

incorruptible as gold,
focused as lightning.
O god of daughters,

guard well this daughter
for this daughter's father's
hand is as weak as the grass,

for his voice is as thin as
the breath in the shepherd's pipe,
and his chest is as narrowly small

as the breast of the sparrow,
for his thighs are as slender
as the reeds by the riverbank,

and the gaze of his eye
is doubtful and dim
and lost in the dark.

HONEYSUCKLE

By the road at the bottom of the driveway,
you pick honeysuckle flowers,
pluck the white, silk-smooth, heart-shaped petals,
strew them on the ground at your feet.
You tell me to do the same, so I pick the honeysuckle
flowers, pluck the white, silk-smooth, heart-shaped petals,
strew them on the ground with yours.
I marvel at how much you have grown in a year.
You are tall as a yardstick.
You can reach all of the doorknobs,
most of the light switches, half of the faucets.
I grunt now when I pick you up.
But it is another summer I am thinking of,
one as far off as another planet,
but one that will arrive as swift as an arrow
toward the heart, as straight as an arrow into the heart,
when you are at the bottom of the driveway,
by the road, with a boy your age or a little older,
and you pick honeysuckle flowers,
pluck the petals, strew them on the ground at your feet.
You tell him to do the same, so he picks the honeysuckle
flowers, plucks the petals, strews them
on the ground with yours,
white, silk-smooth, little hearts.

SWIMMING LESSONS

Your hair is plastered to your head.
Your pigtails drip,
two black icicles in the sun.

You wipe water from your face and eyes
with one hand. With the other,
you grip the handhold.

You wait for your turn to float
on your back or stomach
or kick with the yellow board.

You are small there
up to your shoulders in the water,
but you are not afraid.

Daughter, listen carefully.
No matter what you may read,
or what you may hear,

this water is not a metaphor for life,
nor is this lesson one for learning how to live.
Daughter, listen more carefully.

I am about to contradict myself.
One day you will wipe life from your face
and eyes. With the other,

you will grip the handhold.
One day you will wait your turn
to float on your back or stomach,

or kick with the yellow board.
One day you will be small there,
up to your shoulders in it,

but you will not be afraid.
Now, listen most carefully of all.
I say you will not be afraid.

from *Beautiful Day*   2015

I OFTEN WALK TO THE END OF THE ROAD

I often walk to the end of the road
to look at the abandoned farm.

I like to look at the field
as it goes back to wilderness again.

I like to look at the grass grow
higher and thicker around the barn,

embrace it with its hairy arms
as though welcoming back the wood.

I like to look at the barn turn more
and more gray. It sags in the middle.

It reminds me of the last old horse
that years ago stood as still as a barn.

I like to watch the earth at work.
So slowly, so patiently, so deliberately

the earth works. I like to watch
the earth turn the blue farm machines

to brown rust, turn the red farm
machines to brown rust, turn

the green farm machines to brown rust.
I like to look at her work with metal,

which is mortal like us. "No hurry,"
the earth smiles at me as I watch

her work. How gentle she is
with them, with the hay wain,

with the tractor, with the plow.
"No hurry," she smiles. "No hurry."

THE END OF HISTORY

It was December seventh.
I asked them if they knew the significance of the date.
One said the semester's almost over.
Another said 18 shopping days 'til Christmas.
A third said it's your birthday.
No, I said. No, I said. No, I said.
Then a fourth one said it's Pearl Harbor.
Yes, I said.
The same one said when the kamikazes sank our ships.
No, I said.
There were no kamikazes at Pearl Harbor, I said
They weren't used until later, when Japan was losing, I said.
When they were almost all out of pilots and planes, I said.
The same one said then how did they sink our ships?
The same one said if they didn't crash their planes into them?
I drew a cartoon aircraft carrier on the board.
I drew cartoon dive bombers flying from the cartoon ship to a
cartoon Hawaii.
I drew cartoon torpedo planes flying to the cartoon Hawaii.
I drew cartoon bombs falling on our cartoon ships.
I drew cartoon torpedoes blowing up our cartoon ships.
This is how, I said.
So this is how history ends.
So that bastard Bush was right.
Nine-eleven really did change everything.

THE PATH

A spring-like day in Autumn.
November tries warmth on
and it fits. On the common,
a flag football game.

A girlfriend watches
her small town hero
run his predetermined zero
into the green patches.

I circle around the players,
shift my bag from hand to hand.
They do not understand
what the past is. The future,

too, is a mystery to them.
To these, time is nothing.
To me, everything.
They ride the pendulum.

I count each swing,
perpetually, back and forth.
I hasten along the arcing path
and look up without looking.

To know what will happen
never makes what happens easier.
The ash leaves seek one another
on the ground, to form again,

in the path's curve, an ash tree,
and on the lawn of Morrison Hall
the brown and red leaves fall,
and in front of the library

maples get lost in light.
The faces blur into one face,
and the names, without a trace,
disappear overnight.

I see myself in the glass
of the door, a shadow, hurled
through the zero of the world.
Harmless, I pass

in, to disengage,
to read the maples lost
in light, to read the frost
coming on, to read a page

or two, to read the man
looking back in the glass
like a book I read once
and since have forgotten.

A DIALOGUE WITH MY DAUGHTER THROUGH THE WINDOW OF HER DOLLHOUSE

"The days never end, but people end, right?"
My daughter asks me this today. Dazed
by her question, my mind goes blank. I stare.
Then I say, "Yes, people end. All people end
when they're old. It's called death. Days never
end, though, because days are not people

who have blood and bones and skin and..." "Never
mind," she says, going back to the people
in her dollhouse, bending their arms, the right
leg, the left leg, to seat each one in a chair.
But this explanation will not be the end
of it. I know there will be other days,

tomorrow perhaps, when she will take me unaware
with, "Why do people end? Will Mommy end?
Will you end? Will I end?" So I'll have to get it right.
I'll have to clear my throat, sigh as wise people
sigh before I say, "Emily, you must never
doubt that God made people end to fill the endless days

in Heaven." Then she'll ask about Heaven, and right
away I'll be in trouble because I'll never
be convincing about a place where people
have wings and play harps, a place without days
and nights, or of just one day without end.
Even if satisfied with that, she'll want to know where

it is and about God and what gives God the right
to make us do anything he pleases, as though people
were dolls and the world a dollhouse. At my wit's end,
I'll probably blurt out something I'll regret for days,
such as, "God's like a person, but we really can't compare
God to a person because God, you know, will never

end as people do." To which she'll say, "So the days
are like God then because the days don't end
either, right Dad?" I will smile in despair.
I will smile and nod and hope she never
asks again. I will watch her play with her people,
watch her bend their wooden heads to the left and the right.

SMOKING

I miss the first cigarette of the day,
the one before both eyes are open,
the one before shaving,
the one before showering,
the one before dressing,
the one before breakfast.
I miss the smoke that rises to the ceiling
like mist on a lake in the mountains.
I miss the cigarette after breakfast,
the one with the coffee.
I miss the second cigarette with the coffee.
I miss the cigarette in the car,
my left arm dangling out the window.
I miss guessing how long the ash will hold
before falling off while I'm stopped at a red light.
I miss the cigarette in the men's room.
I miss the hiss of the cigarette butt
as it hits the bowl water.
I miss the cigarettes at lunch
and the round black ashtrays on the table.
I miss the cigarettes at work
and the square glass ashtray on the desk.
I miss my Zippo lighter.
I miss holding it in my hand,
opening and closing it.
I miss the soft click it made when it opened,
and I miss the sharp click it made when it snapped shut.
I miss rubbing my Zippo lighter with my thumb.
I miss the real smooth stainless steel feel.
I miss lighting a stranger's cigarette with it on the street.
I miss the flawless flame of my Zippo lighter.
I miss feeling smooth.
I miss saying the word *Zippo... Zippo...Zippo.*

I miss the last cigarette of the day,
the one just before going to bed,
the one you least enjoy,
the one you don't even know you had.

BANKS

In the Chase Manhattan Bank branch
on the corner of 235th Street
and Johnson Avenue, I have changed
my mind about banks. I never used
to like banks. I despised banks. Now
I like banks. I like standing in the cool
lobbies of banks. I like the brass stanchions
and the velvet ropes that are swagged
between them that you must follow
to the tellers' windows, as though through
a maze. I like the ballpoint pens chained
to the counters where you fill out deposit
slips and withdrawal slips. I like the blue
deposit slips and the pink withdrawal slips.
I like the look on the faces of the tellers,
especially when there are many customers
waiting. They are the concentrated faces
of efficiency. I like to say something
pleasant and polite and civil to the tellers
when it is my turn at the window.
Their gratitude is palpable. It shows on
their efficient faces, and I like that.
I like being a number. I like being several
numbers. I never thought I'd like being
a number, but I do. I like being a number
and a face without a name. It is such
a pleasure not having a name for a little
while during the day. How tiring it is
to answer to a name all the time. I like
the air-conditioned, clean smell of banks.
I like the brand new bills they give me.
I like the way they smell and feel and look.
They remind me of the brand new

books they gave me in school, that I was
the first to use. I like the word. I like
the sound of the word "bank." It's the sound
the vault makes when it's shut and locked.
I like to look at the big vault door. I like
the shiny brushed steel of it. I like
the solidity of it, the indestructibility.
I like the enormous tumblers of the locks.
I like the timing mechanism in its glass
case. I like the handle, big as the handle
on the air-lock of a submarine. The door
looks strong enough to keep out death,
master-thief, genius of safe-crackers.
I do not like death.

THE SCHOOLS OF POETRY

The first was my elementary school, P.S. 76.
There I learned that poetry
is red roses, blue violets, sweet sugar, and sweet you.

The second was my junior high school, Olinville.
There I learned that poetry
is a yellow wood with two diverging roads.

The third was my high school, Evander Childs.
There I learned that poetry
is the dwelling place of possibility.

The fourth was my college, Herbert H. Lehman.
There I learned that poetry
has a favorite month, April the cruelest.

The fifth was my graduate school, State University of New York.
There I learned that poetry
is a cold eye cast on life, on death, of a horseman passing by.

BEAUTIFUL DAY

It was a beautiful day today.
It was mild. There was a breeze,

firm but gentle. It pushed
the crowns of the trees the way

a father pushes a daughter in a swing.
The rhododendrons were in bloom.

The bees were busy in them.
The peonies were starting to unknot.

The sky was fresh with bright blue.
The clouds were white and soft.

They floated like flowers on the pond
of sky. I heard the song of wrens

as they sang in their house in the beech.
It was beautiful today. My daughter

made beautiful swings in the swing.
My wife made beautiful sounds at the piano.

I thought beautiful things in the chair on the lawn.
It was so beautiful I wanted to scream.

I screamed a long, loud scream.
It had one vowel and no consonants.

Then I screamed a second scream.
Then I screamed a third scream.

Both had one vowel and no consonants.
The telephone rang. It was my neighbor.

He wanted to know if everything was all right.
I said the day was so beautiful I screamed.

He said, *Ah, I understand* and hung up.
A police car arrived. The officer knocked.

He said he got a report of three loud screams.
I said the day was so beautiful I screamed.

He said, *Ah, I understand* and drove away.
A fire truck pulled into my driveway.

Three firemen jumped off. They had axes.
They said they got a call about a fire.

I pointed to my heart. It was burning in my chest.
They could see the glow through my skin.

They said, *Ah, we understand* and left,
leaving me burning and glowing, burning and glowing.

ODE TO COFFEE

Wine of the bean.
Why do I call you wine of the bean?
I call you by your first name.
I call you by your Arabic name.
I call you what they who first knew you called you.
Those were the Sufi mystics.
Copiously they drank you to keep them awake all night for their
    all-night prayers.

Coffee, coffee, coffee.
Three times I lift my cup to you.
With you with you.
Three times you clap your strong black hands in front of me.
Three times squarely in front of my face.
Three times squarely between my half-closed eyelids.

Clap! Clap! Clap!
Three thunderclaps squarely in front of my eyes.
Morning companion.
Unfailing, faithful friend of my kitchen table.
I look deeply into your black-hearted soul.
I see there my own black-hearted dreams.
The black-hearted nightmares of my nights.
What are they?
They are falling off cliffs.
They are drowning in rivers.
They are being pursued by an assassin without a face.

Coffee, coffee, coffee.
I swallow you three times.
And so I consume the living black hearts of my enemies.
And so I assume the great height of the cliff.
So I assume the awesome power of the river.
So I assume the single-mindedness of the assassin without a face.

Coffee, coffee, coffee.
Now let me not forget that you also have enemies.
You also have nightmares.
You also live in the valley of the shadow of death.
Let me not forget there are those who would becloud you with
          milk.
There are those who would befog you with cream.
There are those who would bewilder you with half-and-half.
There are those who would befoul you with the sickliness of
          sugar.
And there are those, even those, who would poison you with the
          sweetness of chemistry.

These things will I never do.
O companion of my morning!
O faithful unfailing friend of my kitchen table!
O blood-brother wine of the bean!
O comrade coffee!

TO MY BEARD

What can I say but I am sorry,
I apologize for what I do to you,
my daily ruthlessness and cruelty.
What can I do but ask for your forgiveness
and your patience. For someday,
I promise you, someday I swear
on the beards of the prophets,
and on the beard of the poet Whitman, and
on the beard of the president Lincoln,
and on the red beard of the grandfather,
I will not stop you any longer,
I will let you go free, I will take down
the fence around you made of sharp blades.
For someday, I promise you, I will let
you run wild through the valleys
of my face like a stallion, I will let you
wander over the desert of my face
like a holy man in his vision of heaven
and hell, I will let you grow, blossom
and flourish, and I will stroke you
and comb you and keep you orderly
and free of knots and tangles,
and you in turn will make me look
distinguished, a wise old man as I stroke
you looking serious, looking as though
I were thinking deep thoughts about
life and death. But I will be thinking
only about you, my beard, my second
face, and this will be our secret.

TO MY THUMBS

So is it you then who
are responsible for me?

Am I all thumbs, after all?
You apposite opposites,

you opposables, do you really
believe you are indisposable?

Don't be so smug.
Don't be so cocksure of yourselves.

Thumbs down, thumbs.
Screw you.

I know of at least one who
could have written this with his left foot.

And of another one who
could have done it with his teeth.

TO MY FEET

Sit up here, feet.
Get a load off.

Come up here on the desk,
across from me at legs' length,

so I can see you,
so I can thank you properly.

I want to thank you properly for
taking me everywhere I have needed to go:

Up the steps of libraries and
down the steps of basement restaurants.

Across the avenues of cities and
across the streets of small towns.

Along the hallways of hospitals
and along the corridors of schools.

On the paths of gardens, the trails of forests,
the sands of beaches, the grass of meadows,

the polished floors of gymnasiums.
Sit up here, feet.

How tired you look.
How weary you must be from carrying me

around on your shoulders all these years.
Rest a while, feet.

Soon enough will people
begin to whisper, hiding their mouths

behind their hands, that I look like
I have one of you in the grave.

TO MY EYES

Runts of the litter, you were always the weakest ones.
You were always the neediest. Right from the start,

in first grade, my mother had to get those heavy glass
crutches for you. How stupid you looked walking around

with them. How embarrassed you were. How helpless
you were without them. That was what the bullies went for first.

How they loved to kick the glass crutches out from under you
and laugh as you froze in place. And the eye doctors were wrong,

the ones who said you would improve, who said that someday
you would not need them anymore. They are lighter now,

it's true, less bulky, more stylish. And even though you need
them more than ever, all in all, things could have been worse.

You have become such talented historians. See how
much more I have learned from the two of you than

I could have learned from a hundred history books,
for you have showed me so vividly, so true-to-life what life

was like a thousand years ago, as I walk the rough roads, my hand
on the shoulder of my daughter or my son, who curses me as I stumble.

TO MY FAVORITE CORDUROY JACKET

Such dust on your shoulders,
beautiful corduroy jacket.
How did you get such dust
on your shoulders? Have you
been holding up the ceiling
of the closet all summer?
I see you are getting old.
I see how thin you are getting.
Soon I will have to replace
the leather patches where
my elbows have worn through.
And your satin lining. What
a mess. You can't even hold
a pen in your inside pocket
anymore. It just falls through
to the floor. Your lapels,
which when I first set eyes on
them, I thought were Pegasus
wings, are gnarled, twisted,
curled, useless as the wings
of an ostrich. At least you have
all your buttons. You're lucky,
although it's true, one's life
is hanging by a thread. How
ironic that is since except
for that one time when I first
put you on, I've never buttoned
you up. I wonder why.
Could it be that I am so shy,
so timid, so uncertain of
my own mind, I always let you
speak for me? I must remember
to tell the undertaker to button
your lip along with mine.

I know I should send you away
to the tailor to be sewn up,
but I'm afraid to send you away.
I also am getting old, and I'm
afraid to be apart from you,
even for just a week. Haven't
I already sworn that I will
die in your arms -- O corduroy
armor – O corduroy critic-proof
vest – that we will become dust
together, that together we will
become dust of corduroy, dust
of man, that we will become
dust of corduroy-man, and together
hold up the ceiling of the closet
of the earth all summer, all fall,
all winter, all spring? Forever?

BEAUTY

From my room down the hall,
I can hear the mathematics
professor getting emotional
about an equation, and I ask
myself how someone can get
so worked up about what isn't real,
an abstraction, nothing but
signs and symbols. A scribble.

Oh, I say to myself. *To him
it is a poem, a formal one,
every word in place, every rhyme
perfect, every stanza exact. Poor man.
He, too, must pound the beauty in
with his fist. Every time. Every damn time.*

from *Heart's Content*   2016

ANGINA

It is a hand on the heart,
a greeting.
It is mortality grinning,
dumbly, with its big,

hearty hand on the heart,
mortality in person,
squeezing the heart
with its big, hot hand.

And then it becomes
remembering,
the heart remembering
painful experiences

from its infancy,
its childhood and its youth,
separations in the dark,
nightmares of falling

and chases through forests,
unrequited love for heroines
of books and movie stars,
an ache in the shape

of a hand holding such
a heavy heart heart-level
and too long to bear.
It is Latin for *torture*.

THE WORLD THROUGH THE GLASS WALL OF THE CARDIOLOGY PAVILION

It is almost the real world.
Mostly sky, almost as blue as it really is.

Clouds toward the bottom, almost as white as they really are.
A foreground of trees almost as green as they really are.

And visible through the gaps,
almost as autonomic, almost as unconscious, almost as natural,

a stream of cars like the blood cells in the artery of your arm.
The real world.

Such a curious place.
Every day the mirrored wall of your dreams dissolves.

Every day it resolves into the glass wall of your world awake.
The real world.

Almost as real as the world as it is.
Almost as real as the dream of the real blood in your real heart.

THE CEILING

It is one sixty-fourth of a chessboard that isn't there.
I am the king of the white square the size of a room.

It is a sky without birds, except for those I remember.
It is a sky without clouds, except for those I remember.

It is the skeleton of the sky.
It is the ice cap at the arctic attic of the house.

It is the screen on which movies are played.
These are the movies that star all the family dead.

It is the white satin lining of the coffin lid.
This is the lid that closes every night upon our lids.

It is the last sky most of us will ever see.
Darkly will we see it through a painless fog.

It is the headroom of hell.
It is the polar route to paradise.

AFTERLIFE

It ought to be a long nap out of doors
some afternoon at the very end of summer,

the first Sunday of September say, perhaps
in the outsized hammock slung between

the two black birch trees out back,
or on the porch, in the chaise without the pillow,

that out of print book of poems open on your chest,
the sun sliding in and out of the clouds,

or best of all, in the old rowboat anchored
out in the middle of the lake, too far out

for all the reasons not to be so far,
the oars overboard, drifting outward,

back to the shoreline you started out from,
parallel, together, an equal sign, way out there.

THE MIND AT NIGHT

Have you noticed, for example,
how at night the mind climbs
the fence into the apple orchard,
boldly, brazenly, vaulting the top,
how it does so without the smallest
sign of hesitation, doubt, or fear,
and without the slightest tremolo
in its voice, cries out aloud for
the world to hear, *Mine, mine, mine!*

TIME

Neither yours
to give

nor mine
to take,

yet so
warm

from
our hands.

from *Won't Be Long* 2016

PATRIOTISM

I don't own an American flag.
I never have.

I grew up in an apartment building in the Bronx.
Nobody owned a flag.

Now that I live on a road in the country,
all my neighbors fly the flag.

Except one.
Like them, he does have a flagpole

with a flag hanging on it
in front of his house.

But he says he isn't flying it.
He says he's lynching it.

HIS NOSE ANSWERS DR. WILLIAMS

No, I cannot be decent.
No, I cannot reserve my ardors
for something less unlovely than that rank
odor of a passing spring.
Yes, I must taste everything!
Yes, I must know everything!
Yes, I must have a part in everything!
And don't worry, Doc.
Flossie will care for us if we continue in these ways.

AS TO WHAT HE HAS DONE

As to what he has done
and what he has not done:
He has taught some things
to some but has left much
more untaught to more.
He has written some words
but has left more unwritten.
Many nights he has not slept
thinking, "What does better mean?"

PRIVATE PROPERTY

There are 57,308,738 square
miles of land in the world.

That's 36,677,592,320 acres.
As decreed by Map16,

Block 2, Lots 3 and 4,
I own 0.50 acres.

This comes to 1/73,355,104,640[th]
of the land in the world.

Keep out.

PHILOSOPHY

The Pythagoreans worshiped number.
They believed that fire was made of 24
right angled triangles surrounded by 4
equilateral triangles composed of 6
right angled triangles. But they thought
about such things only after the water
boiled for the morning coffee.

WALK

"Look, there's a deer skull," I said
pointing to the deer skull by the side of the road.

"Look, there's a beer skull," Jim said
pointing to the Coors can by the side of the road.

ON THE WALL

of one of the stalls
in the men's room,
someone wrote,
"I want my sweater
back." Or perhaps
it was, "I want my
sweetheart back."
It was hard to read.

THE NAMES

One spelled Dickinson with an *e*.
Another spelled Eliot with an extra *l*.
A third spelled Whitman without an *h*.
"If nothing else," I said, "spell the names right."
If nothing else, at least the fucking names, I didn't say.

KNOWLEDGE

Knowing how paper is made,
or how ink is made,

or how a pencil is made,
has nothing to do with

how a poem is made.
How lucky for the poet!

Q & A

Did He who made the lamb make thee?
Yes, He who made the lamb made me.
But made me first, his master stroke.
And then the lamb, his little joke.

THE DIFFERENCES

The differences
between the earth
and the world
are many, but
the only one
you really need
to know is that
the earth rotates
and the world spins.

BEES IN THE WILD CHERRY TREE

In my next life,
I want to come back
as the honey bees.

Yes, you heard me right.
Not one bee.
All of them.

MEANS TO ENDS

Would you make
a better bed of roses

if the only way
to do it was

to make a sharper
crown of thorns?

POEM BASED ON FIVE WORDS GIVEN TO MY
DAUGHTER BY HER FIRST GRADE TEACHER:
LIKE, OUR, PLAY, SAW, WAS

Like me, you are tormented by words.
Our sky is two skies.
Blackbirds play letters in them.
In yours, *saw.*
In mine, *was.*

SOME THINGS

Some things
are just

so crazy
to think about

that we
have no

choice except
to do them

without
thinking.

THE DREAM

In the dream
I was invisible

until I passed
through the world

of invisible mirrors
and saw myself.

THE MORNING FREIGHT

Did you see it?
No?

How well
it covers its tracks.

CONFESSION

I am faithful
to my wife.

And that's
the long

and the
short of it.

QUESTION FOR THE ORACLE

Know thyself.
Okay.

Nothing in excess.
Okay.

But does that include
knowing thyself?

IN POETRY

In poetry, there are
no wrong words.

There are only
sour notes.

APOLOGY

What I had
in mind

is not what
I had in mind.

SIMILE

The good memory
sits heavily

on your mind
like a bad memory.

AGNOSTICISM

I can be
convinced,

but it
will have

to be
in person.

MARCH 14

Today is
Einstein's
birthday.
The sun
is shining.

POSITIONAL

I'm under
no illusions.

I'm over
them.

POST-COITAL

It all
comes
down
to this.

HAMLET

Revenge play
with a vengeance.

PESSIMISM

Time after time after time...

OPTIMISM

Time before time before time...

IN THE TERMINAL

Interminable.

from *Invisible*   2017

BRANDO

He's a box.
He is wrapped in a tee shirt.
The tee shirt is a little too tight.
He wants you to see the shape of the box.

The arms of the box are akimbo.
The right hand of the box is under the left bicep.
The right hand is pushing the left bicep toward you.
That way it looks bigger, more impressive, sexier.

The left eye of the box says, *Open me.*
The right eye of the box says, *If you dare.*
Both eyes of the box say, *Look but do not touch.*
The box has a nose, but it is made of putty.

The box has a mouth, but it is painted on.
The box has a forehead.
The forehead looks like a third bicep.
Or does the box want his biceps to resemble two foreheads?

The box is bulging his forehead at you.
He does this by looking out from under his boxy brows.
He wants you to know there is a brain in there.
He wants you to know it is a big brain, a sexy brain.

He wants you to know his brain is bigger than yours.
He wants you to know his brain is sexier than yours.
So he points it at you, his forehead.
It is the same as telling you his biceps are bigger than yours.

This box wants you to understand something.
He wants you to understand he can beat you any way he wants.
He can beat you with his biceps.
He can beat you with his brains.

Other than that, it is hard to tell what this box wants.
It is a mystery box.
It is a heavy box.
It is an empty box.

BRUCE SPRINGSTEEN'S GUITAR

is white
is pure white
is pure dominant, pure tonic

is white
is snow, is ice
is a glacier glissando

is white
is a swan
is a swan with a straight-as-an-arrow neck

is white
is lily white
is a lily pressed and dried in a book

is white
is a white whale white
is Ahab caught in the web of strings

is white
is white hot
is dead white, dead-center white

is white
is bridal gown white
is the bride of rock and roll

is white
is ghost white
is the ghost of a blue guitar

E. D. AT THE ACADEMY

In School --
I was rebellious.

I was a No Hoper --
The Headmistress

gave me a Job -- to wipe
the Knives in the dining hall.

Only the Knives --
Nothing else --

But I Wiped -- a Spoon
or Two behind her Back --

And a Fork once.
I left after a Year --

I had Learned everything
they had to teach.

As for Grammar --Well --
Dash it All!

EINSTEIN'S LAST WORDS

(Einstein's last words were never preserved
because he spoke them in German, which the
attending nurse did not understand.)

Surely it must have been a simple thing,
that sort of phrase the ordinary old
might say, child-like, such as "More light" or "Bring
me, please, water" or "Close the door" or "Hold

my hand" or "I was wrong" or "What's the time?"
Perhaps it was a line or two of verse
from *Faust* or a nonsense nursery rhyme
that curved around to close his universe.

But if all he said was a little joke,
of a man meeting God in Paradise,
and God laughed once, even then, he spoke
to himself. Both silences must suffice.

FOUND POEM WITH VARIATIONS

Paganini is supposed to have said
that Stradivari "only used the wood
on trees on which nightingales sang."

Frost is supposed to have said
that Dickinson "only used the paper
from trees on which butterflies were born."

Pound is supposed to have said
that Whitman "only used the paper
from trees under whose boughs couples copulated."

Moore is supposed to have said
that Frost "only used the paper
from New Hampshire maple trees."

Tennyson is supposed to have said
that Blake "only used the paper
from trees in which angels sat."

Creeley is supposed to have said
that Ginsberg "only used the paper
from the same trees Whitman used."

QUAKER GATHERING FOR ALICE

It is simple.
In the center of the room is a table.
A candle is on the table.
A vase is on the table.

In the vase are yellow daffodils.
In the vase are white daffodils.
It is spring.
They burn yellow like yellow candles.

They burn white like white candles.
Sunlight shines through the windows.
The windows burn white.
The walls of the room are white.

We who are quietly gathered
quietly remember her.
We who are softly gathered
softly remember her.

She was simple.
For ninety-five years she was a candle.
For ninety-five years
the storms could not extinguish her.

For ninety-five years she was simple.
Now she is simpler still.
She is simpler than candles.
She is simpler than flowers.

She is simpler than years.
She is simpler than windows,
than sunlight through windows.
She is simple.

IN THE HOUSE OF SALT

In the house of salt, every window is an open wound.
In the house of fire, there is no light.

In the house of dreams, there is no rest.
In the house of women, there is no opportunity.

In the house of steel, there is no need for iron.
In the house of laughter, there is no need for jokes.

In the house of ice, there is nothing to drink.
In the house of the moon, the sun is the devil.

In the house of nightmares, there is no mercy.
In the house of butterflies, moths are not welcome.

In the house of mirrors, your face is your life's work.
In the house of piety, there is not enough pity to go around.

In the house of toys, there is no need for wisdom.
In the house of bells, there is no need for conversation.

In the house of heroes, the story of the coward gets longer
    with every telling.
In the house of hell, only the ceiling is fireproof.

In the house of the sky, you must never look down.
In the house of circles, there is no need to think straight.

In the house of the future, you will live like there is no today.
In the house of the valley, your dreams are the echoes of your days.

In the house of numbers, all names end with a question mark.
In the house of rain, you reach your destiny by river only.

In the house of history, you will carry 10,000 flags.
In the house of honey, only silk flowers may be arranged
     in the vases.

In the house of wolves, who will tell the bedtime stories?
In the house of hours, minutes are your parents, seconds are
     your grandparents.

In the house of clocks, calendars are holy scripture.
In the house of nails, not forever can you hide your hammer.

In the house of hawks, you must perfect the art of disguise.
In the house of music, there are more secrets than keepers of
     secrets.

In the house of courage, there is no need for fathers.
In the house of books, there is no need for doors.

In the house of miracles, magic is strangled in the cradle.
In the house of dance, only the crippled may walk.

In the house of roses, where do the daisies sleep?
In the house of hair, the comb hangs over the fireplace and the
     razor blades are bronzed.

In the house of sunshine, the shadows never lose their edge.
In the house of prayer, the cries of the hungry go unheeded.

In the house of comedy, the worst of tragedies is silence.
In the house of hope, the light switches read *on* and *on*.

In the house of lost causes, the soapboxes are in the garage,
     neatly stacked.
In the house of flattery, how do you know which one to imitate?

In the house of happy endings, the sadder the beginning the better.
In the house of impossibilities, forty times forty is not time enough.

In the house of strong opinions, the facts are the first to leave the
    room and the last to return.
In the house of mistaken identities, all love is irksome.

In the house of secrets, blackmail is for breakfast.
In the house of hypocrisy, the name on the mailbox is *Politics*.

In the house of paradox, the poet is always welcome.
In the house of poetry, truth lives in the basement, language in the attic.

In the house of certainty, the foundation rests on the skulls
    of the mistaken.
In the house of dust, death feels right at home.

INVISIBLE

1.
When they are thirteen, all boys want to be invisible.

2.
The physicists tell us ninety percent of the universe is invisible.

3.
Should it not occur to us that since the greatest part of our lives
is lived in our minds, we too are ninety percent invisible?

4.
When we watch the willow branches stirred by the wind,
when we watch the cumulus clouds billow in the wind,
when we watch the paper kite strain the string in the wind,
three times we ponder the invisible.

5.
Of all the incredible things about my cat Hector,
the most incredible is how he sees the invisible.

6.
Except when it is reflecting something else, glass,
the most miraculous of materials, so too the most
metaphorical, is naturally visibly invisible.

7.
And then there is godmother death, her gray hair,
her false teeth, her cane, whom we know from birth,
so familiar to us she is all but invisible.

SHAKER CHAIR

Ballerina of a chair.
Chair *en point.*
Chair on tip-toe to be taller.
Thin-as-a-rail, anorexic chair.

Haiku chair.
Pure and simple chair, pure and simple.
Lithe chair.
Light chair, lighter than air.

Shrewd chair.
Stern chair.
Stiff, stiff-necked chair.
No nonsense chair.

Chair straight to the point of its four points.
Chair all business of going about
its father's business
of form following function following faith.

Austere chair.
Such soft-spoken austerity.
Severe chair.
Such soft-spoken severity.

Discreet chair.
The very soul of discretion.
Stick figure chair
for the stick figure father to sit in.

Secret chair.
Open chair.
Open secret of chairs.
Spare chair with nothing to spare.

THE HORSES

Eight million died in World War I.

They would have needed 8,000,000 men
for one man to apologize to one horse.

It would have taken 8,000,000 Picassos
to do justice to the death agony of 8,000,000 horses.

Of the 8,000,000 horses, how many had names?
The Germans in particular targeted the horses.

When a British soldier's was killed or died,
he was required to cut off a hoof from his horse

to prove to his commanding officer that they
had not simply been separated, he and his horse.

Too tired to lift their heads high enough to breathe,
they drowned in the deep mud, thousands of the horses.

Because they were used to draw the artillery,
the most losses were suffered by the Clydesdale horses.

For some countries, the largest commodity
shipped to the front was fodder for the horses.

Because saw dust was mixed with their food,
they starved to death, thousands of the horses.

Gasmasks were issued for the horses,
but they destroyed them, mistaking them for feed bags.

The better-bred horses suffered from shell shock
more than the less well-bred horses.

These learned to lie down at the sound of the guns.
They were sold to the French butchers, the surviving horses.

THE LOVER OF STONE

The lover of stone must be old,
for there is no such thing as a young stone.

The lover of stone must be strong,
for he must able to climb up the mountain

and the summit of the mountain
to find the beginning of stone.

And he must be able to climb down
the mountain again to the valley

and to the bottom of the valley
to find the ending of stone.

The lover of stone must be a genius at unrequited love.
He must be an connoisseur of the cold.

The lover of stone must be a saint,
for stone will no more return his love

than does God return that of the saint.
The lover of stone must be jealous.

He must be jealous of the water that loves stone to smooth.
And he must be jealous of the wind that loves stone to death.

THE POEM OF THE FUTURE

The poem of the future will be smaller.
It will fit in the palm of your hand,
on your wrist, in your ear.

The poem of the future will not need
bulky batteries or cumbersome wires.
It will be powered by moonlight and weed.

The poem of the future will be automatic.
It will go for months without routine maintenance.
It will be faster, smoother, with a digital tick.

The poem of the future will be lighter.
It will be made of plastics and exotic metals.
It will be available in hundreds of shapes and colors.

The poem of the future will make our lives true.
It will perform in a second what it takes
the poem of the present a day to do.

The poem of the future will talk to us.
It will say things like "Buy IBM," and "Friend me,"
and "Pulvis et umbra sumus."

WORSE

One could do worse than be a swinger of birches.

For example, one could be a slinger of burgers at McDonald's.
Or one could be a bringer of frivolous lawsuits.
Or one could be a flinger of gossipy dirt for *The New York Post.*

Or one could be a singer of inane songs on MTV for pre-teens.
Or one could be a clinger of apron strings.
Or one could be a dead-ringer for one of the FBI's *Ten Most Wanted.*

Or one could be a hunch-backed ringer of French church bells.
Or one could be a second-stringer on a last place minor
        league baseball team.
Or one could be a stringer for a newspaper in the sticks.

Or one could be a finger man for the mafia.
Or one could be a dinger of car fenders in the parking lot of Walmart.
Or one could be a left-winger for a last place minor league
        hockey team.

Or one could be a right-winger of any country's politics.
Or one could be a jingler of idiotic jingles on the radio for pre-teens.
Or one could be a malingerer.

23 ATTEMPTS AT THE WILLIAM MATTHEWS CHALLENGE TO RUIN, WITH THE LEAST POSSIBLE CHANGE, A FAMOUS LINE OF POETRY

1.

Whose woods these are I think I know.

Whose irons these are I think I know.

2.

I heard a Fly Buzz – when I died –

I heard a Fly Buzz – when it died –

3.

The proper study of mankind is Man.

The proper study of mankind is jazz, man.

4.

Let us go then, you and I

Let us go then, me and you

5.

Little Lamb, who made thee?

Little Goat, who made thee?

6.
In Xanadu did Kubla Khan

In Timbuktu did Kubla Khan

7.
When I was one and twenty

When I was twenty-one

8.
I caught a tremendous fish

I caught a whopper

9.
"O where ha' you been, Lord Randall, my son?"

"O where ha' you been, Lord Sheldon, my son?"

10.
When I heard the learn'd astronomer

When I heard the learn'd astrologer

11.
About suffering they were never wrong

About surfing they were never wrong

12.
A poem should be palpable and mute

A poem should be palpable and cute

13.
Drink to me only with thine eyes

Blink to me only with thine eyes

14.
I felt a Funeral, in my Brain

I felt a Funeral, in my Spleen

15.
There were three ravens sat on a tree

There were three mavens sat on a tree.

16.
When I see birches bend to left and right

When I see bitches bend to left and right

17.
Two roads diverged in a yellow wood

Two toads diverged in a yellow wood

18.
O Rose, thou art sick!

O Nose, thou art sick!

19.
Something there is that doesn't love a wall

Something there is that doesn't love a mall

20.
Gather ye rose-buds while ye may

Gather ye nose-bugs while ye may

21.
Do not go gentle into that goodnight

Do not go, gentile, into that goodnight

22.
How do I love thee? Let me count the ways.

How do I love thee? Let me count the lays.

23.
I wandered lonely as a cloud

I wondered, "Lonely as a cloud?"

OVER THERE

Although we know they may
not be better necessarily,
over there we know at least
things are different, and we

sense we would be different
ourselves all these years
had we been born, brought
up, nurtured over there,

been given opportunities
to play the barefoot games,
had we had the friends
with the perfect trochee names

who lived on streets with
no sharp corners but with trees
that grew, merged over roads,
melded light like arches,

in houses shadowed with
pianos and portraits in oil,
who went to the alabaster
school on the low, smooth hill

with a library on whose
shelves are only first editions
bound in leather and halls
echoing a bronze tradition

like a language stranger
than ours, older and stronger,
the language of flawless children
into which ours fades forever.

SCHOPENHAUER AT THE ENGLISCHER HOF
A Monologue

I have been called a pessimist. I am.
What man who calls himself a thoughtful man,
a feeling man, can be ought else? The wine?
The wine is good, but I prefer the beer.
I took no wife because I wanted none.
I live alone because I wish to live
alone. The passions must be overcome.
I recommend the veal. It's excellent.
The monarchs made a mockery of hope.
My father was a businessman. He killed
himself when I was seventeen. I left
my mother's house soon afterward because
she chose a life I could not tolerate
to look upon. She was a novelist,
you know, received the intellectuals
of Weimar in her parlor. And her bed.
She let old Goethe bring his Christiane
with him, but when he told her I, her son,
would be a very famous man, she pushed
me down the stairs. Her name is only known
through me, the bitch. Who reads her novels now?
I come to dine here almost every day.
Before I start I place a coin – this one –
beside the plate, and when I'm done, I put
the coin back in my pocket once again.
It is a wager that I've made myself
to drop it in the poor box of the church
the day the English officers who dine
at this establishment should talk of else
than horses, women, or dogs. Here, I have
one. His name is *Atma*. It means World-Soul.
Why was my masterpiece unrecognized?
Because just those who could have given it

publicity – the university
philosophers – I have attacked in it.
Ah, yes, good man, the veal for both of us.
The rule, *I sing the song of him whose bread
I eat,* has always held. It now, too, holds.
I make no living from philosophy.
I have inherited an interest in
my father's firm, and that has been enough.
The life of every individual,
when we survey it as a whole and stress
its most important parts, is tragedy.
But in the details, always comedy.
The world is bankrupt in the end, and life's
a business which does not recoup expense.
All happiness requires ignorance
or youth, for youth and ignorance are one.
The fear of death is the beginning of
philosophy, religion's final cause.
Diogenes refused to breathe – and died.
A brilliant victory! Alas, how vain.
The more things change, the more they stay the same.
This is the essence of philosophy.
The true philosophy of history
lies in perceiving this eternal truth.
In general, the wise have always said
the same. The fools have acted all alike
as well and done the opposite. And thus
reality is suffering and pain.
And thus the genius suffers most of all.
You hear? You hear the English gentlemen?
The coin is in my pocket once again.

ZEPPO

They say he was the funniest
of the four. We'll never know.

In an early film (perhaps to test
just how far they would let him go),

he ad-libs a joke. Groucho,
visibly annoyed, throws a snap

at him as he walks off. At best
he was handsome and sang. A trap.

Invariably they would merely send
him away. But he got the girl in the end.

from *The Black Birch* 2017

THE BLACK BIRCH

A year after the black birch tree
in the backyard died, the tree man
asked me what I wanted to do.
He had come to estimate the cost
of tree work, pruning some oaks,
cutting away dead branches, etc.
We had already decided to try
to save the ash tree in front
rather than cut it down as its
companion had already been.
I thought about it for a little while
and then said, "No, don't take it down.
Let it stand there as it is."
"But it will fall anyway, branch
by branch, twig by twig.
You'll be cleaning up out here often."
"That's all right," I said.
"Let it stand. The birds will use it."
"And the insects," the tree man added.
And the birds have used it, as have
the insects, and I, too, have used it
in my way, picking up branches
and twigs, branches and twigs.

FROZEN ROSE

It's gone today, the frozen rose
I saw yesterday at the top of the otherwise
barren rosebush by the door of the gardener's shed.

Had I not known it was once red,
I would not know the color the frozen rose was,
for it was faded to neutral,

paled down to less than less than brown,
to less than yellowy beige.
White ones, too, turn that non-color color.

Yet it held on, solitary, there at the top of the rosebush,
as though carved from ivory and yellowed with years.
Or created of folded, wrinkled tissue paper

by a master maker of paper roses who,
disappointed in love, made it dead,
made it the color of his frozen heart.

JAPANESE WATER IRIS

The directions say to dig
a hole three times the width
of the root ball. Which I do.
The directions say to place
the plant so that it rests just
above ground level. Which
I do. The directions say to fill
the hole with potting mix.
Which I do. The directions say
to soak until the soil settles.
Which I do. The directions
say to not tamp down. Which
I don't do. The directions say
to add more potting mix if
necessary. Which I do. The
directions do not say to say
a prayer. But I do: *Live, you
skinny purple bastard, live.*

RAKING AT DUSK

There is just enough light
to finish the backyard.
The leaves, wet from all
the rain, are heavy,
but not hard to pick up,
and I get more
in the big garbage pail.
Their oranges, browns and
reds are dark, even somber.
My daughter helps a little.
I think of the Hopkins poem
that begins, *Margaret,*
Are you grieving / over
Goldengrove unleaving?
But this is Blooming Grove,
this girl is Emily, and she
is doing cartwheels in
the dead leaves, her body
a five-pointed leaf,
turning, leaving me
in the dark, believing in life.

No.
In life believing.

THE CACTUS IN THE GREENHOUSE

The cactus in the greenhouse
has three arms.

At the end of one arm,
there is a broad, flat, open

palm of a hand,
with slender spikes for fingers.

It holds up against the pane,
triumphantly,

a single pink flower
so translucent

it looks to be made itself
of pink glass.

"See," says the cactus,
"what I have had to do

to get to the sun.
I have had to make love to glass."

THE ONLY DEFINITION OF POETRY YOU'LL EVER NEED

"Poetry," said the poet
from Brooklyn, "is that
sort of writing you can
read silently to yourself,
on the train or the bus,
while moving your lips
and not be embarrassed."

THE ONLY HAIKU YOU'LL EVER NEED

Issa

It means "cup of tea,"
which for most he is not. O,
unfortunately.

THE ONLY EROTIC POEM YOU'LL EVER NEED

Eros backwards
is sore.

THE ONLY INSOMNIA POEM YOU'LL EVER NEED

Perfect.
The moon one night past full.

The snow gleaming
between silver and white.

Like the paper I cannot sleep in.
Like the bed I cannot write on.

THE BEST NAMES IN POETRY

Russell Banks
Coleman Barks
Ellen Bass

Marvin Bell
Wendell Berry
Elizabeth Bishop

David Bottoms
Robert Bridges
Gwendolyn Brooks

Basil Bunting
Robert Burns
Kelly Cherry

Wendy Cope
Hart Crane
Stephen Crane

Rita Dove
Edward Field
Carol Frost

Robert Frost
Oliver Goldsmith
Robert Graves

Thomas Gray
Barbara Guest
Edgar Guest

Donald Hall
Thomas Hood
Donald Justice

Alicia Keys
Etheridge Knight
Thomas Lux

David Mason
Edgar Lee Masters
Howard Moss

Thylias Moss
Octavio Paz
Molly Peacock

Thomas Love Peacock
Alexander Pope
Ezra Pound

John Crowe Ransom
David Ray
Henry Reed

Ishmael Reed
Adrienne Rich
Robert Service

Anne Sexton
Tom Sleigh
Christopher Smart

Cathy Song
Gerald Stern
Ruth Stone

Mark Strand
Jonathan Swift
Madeline Tiger

Jean Valentine
Robert Penn Warren
Yvor Winters

THE MOVIE OF THIS POEM

For the movie of this poem,
I want James Dean
and Martin Sheen

to play
the masculine rhymes.
For the feminine

rhymes, I want
Bridgette Bardot
and Marilyn Monroe.

For the role
of the accented syllables,
I want Richard Burton.

John Gielgud
must play
the caesuras.

I don't know
about the music,
but Ingmar Bergman

or Stanley Kubrik
will have to direct.
Never mind all that.

A silent film.
In black and white.
With Chaplin and a dog.

#1670

Emily, Emily, Emily, your one
thousand six hundred seventieth
poem is such a strange poem, even
for you, Mistress of Strange Poems.
It is the one in which you come
upon, in a dream as you say, a worm,
"pink, lank, and warm,"
which you leash with a piece of string
to your bedpost to keep it from wandering.
You leave for a while, and when
you return later, you find the worm
transformed into a snake, but "ringed
with power." You interview
the worm-snake until it fathoms you.
Yes, Emily, that is your word, "fathoms."
And then you run out of the room,
and out of the house, and out of town,
only to claim, in the very last line,
as I said before, "This was a dream."
Mistress of Strange Dreams, I'm not so sure.
Mistress of Slant, I wonder.

WHENEVER I GET HOME

Whenever I get home
after an exceptionally good day
in class, and I am smug
and full of myself, I am smug
and full of my own voice,
and I am still giddy
from how well it went,
from how articulate I was,
from how my one-liners zipped
along the rows around
the heads like hummingbirds,
I sit down in the uncomfortable
metal chair behind the house
in the shade of the trees,
and I close my eyes and remember
what William Stafford wrote,
Like a little stone, feel
the shadow of the great earth,
and the stupid grin wipes itself
off my stupid face, and then
wipes off my stupid face.

ELEGY FOR A HOUSE FINCH KILLED AGAINST THE WINDOW GLASS

If words can be a grave,
then let these be yours.
I will try to make them
at least as soft as the fresh
dead leaves fallen onto
the bed of myrtle, the place
where I have placed you
to pass the winter. Let all
be soft now. We are both
to blame, I more so than
you. Let me speak softly.
So much of the world is
so hard. At times, too much.
If words can be soft,
let them be these. Or if these
be too hard, let two be soft
enough for you, or one,
just one, like leaves.

from *I, Emily Dickinson & Other Found Poems* 2018

I, EMILY DICKINSON

#1
I am afraid to own a body
I am alive I guess
I am ashamed, I hide
I asked no other thing

I bet with every wind that blew
I breathed enough to take the trick
I bring an unaccustomed wine
I came to buy a smile today

I can wade grief
I cannot be ashamed
I cannot buy it, 'tis not sold
I cannot dance upon my toes

I cannot live with you
I cannot meet the spring unmoved
I cannot see my soul but know 'tis there
I cannot want it more

#2
I can't tell you but you feel it
I cautious scanned my little life
I could bring you jewels had I a mind to
I could die to know

I could not drink it, sweet
I could not prove the years had feet
I could suffice for him, I knew
I counted till they danced so

I cried at pity, not at pain
I cross till I am weary
I did not reach thee
I died for beauty, but was scarce

I dreaded that first robin so
I dwell in possibility
I envy seas whereon he rides
I fear a man of frugal speech

#3
I felt a cleaving in my mind
I felt a funeral in my brain
I felt my life with both my hands
I fit for them – I seek the dark

I found the words to every thought
I gained it so
I gave myself to him
I got so I could take his name

I groped for him before I knew
I had a daily bliss
I had a guinea gold
I had been hungry all the years

I had no cause to be awake
I had no time to hate
I had not minded walls
I had some things that I called mine

#4
I had the glory – that will do
I have a bird in spring
I have a king who does not speak
I have never seen "Volcanoes"

I have no like but this
I haven't told my garden yet
I heard a fly buzz when I died
I heard as if I had no ear

I held a jewel in my fingers
I hide myself within my flower
I keep my pledge
I knew that I had gained

I know a place where summer strives
I know lives, I could miss
I know of people in the grave
I know some lonely houses off the road

#5
I know suspense – it steps so terse
I know that he exists
I know where wells grow, droughtless wells
I learned at least what home could be

I like a look of agony
I like to see it lap the miles
I live with him, I see his face
I lived on dread

I lost the world the other day
I made slow riches but my gain
I make his crescent fill or lack
I many times thought peace had come

I meant to find her when I came
I meant to have but modest needs
I measure every grief I meet
I met a king this afternoon

#6
I never felt at home below
I never hear that one is dead
I never hear the word "escape"
I never lost as much but twice

I never saw a moor
I never told the buried gold
I noticed people disappeared
I often passed the village

I pay in satin cash
I play at riches to appease
I prayed at first a little girl
I read my sentence steadily

I reason earth is short
I reckon when I count at all
I robbed the woods
I rose because he sank

#7
I saw no way – the heavens were stitched
I saw that the flake was on it
I saw the wind within her
I see thee better in the dark

I see thee clearer for the grave
I send two sunsets
I send you a decrepit flower
I shall keep singing

I shall know why, when time is over
I shall not murmur if at last
I should have been too glad, I see
I should not dare to be so sad

I should not dare to leave my friend
I showed her heights she never saw
I sing to use the waiting
I sometimes drop it, for a quick

#8
I started early, took my dog
I stepped from plank to plank
I stole them from a bee
I sued the news, yet feared the news

I suppose the time will come
I taste a liquor never brewed
I tend my flowers for thee
I think I was enchanted

I think just how my shape will rise
I think that the root of the wind is water
I think the hemlock likes to stand
I think the longest hour of all

I think to live may be a bliss
I thought that nature was enough
I thought the train would never come
I tie my hat, I crease my shawl

#9
I took my power in my hand
I took one draught of life
I tried to think a lonelier thing
"I want" – it pleaded all its life

I was a phoebe, nothing more
I was the slightest in the house
I watched her face to see which way
I watched the moon around the house

I went to heaven
I went to thank her
I worked for chaff and earning wheat
I would distil a cup

I would not paint a picture
I years had been from home

(From the index to *The Complete Poems of Emily Dickinson,* Ed. Thomas H. Johnson, Little Brown and Co., 1960)

PERFUME POEM

Manifesto. Eau de Cartier. Mambo.
Beautiful. Lolita Lempicka. Tommy Girl.
Bulgari Pour Femme. Amarige. Opium.

Romance. L'air du Temps. Indecence.
Shalimar. Vera Wong. J'Adore.
Hugo Boss. White Diamonds. Strenesse.

Curve for Women. Organza. Boucheron.
Clinique Happy. Chanel No 5. Eternity.
Light Blue. Cashmere Mist. So You.

(From advertisements in several issues of the *New York Times Sunday Magazine*, dates unknown)

FOUR TREES

Eastern Hemlock

The leaves fall upon drying.
A poor Christmas tree.
Poor quality of wood.

Stone-like hardness of the knots
will chip steel blades.
Lumber taken for pulp.

Useful for railroad ties.
Holds spikes exceptionally well.
Bark rich in tannin.

A tea was once made from leaves
and twigs by woodsmen and Indians.
As fuel, the wood throws sparks.

Japanese Honeysuckle

Fruits eaten
by birds and mammals

and the dense cover
is much used,

but generally speaking
it is a weed.

Smooth Blackhaw

Fruits eaten
by foxes,

bobwhites,
and several

songbirds.
Some people

also like them

Bullbrier Greenbrier

Some twigs
may be

without
prickles.

(From *A Field Guide to Trees and Shrubs, 2nd Edition* by George
A. Petrides, 1972)

DEAD PIANOS

The Knabe baby grand
did a cartwheel and landed
on its back,
legs poking into the air.

A Lester upright
thudded onto its side
with a final groan of strings,
a death-rattling chord.

After 10 pianos were dumped,
a small yellow loader
with a claw in front scuttled
in like a vicious beetle,

crushing keyboards,
soundboards
and cases
into a pile.

(From "For More Pianos, Last Note Is Thud in the Dump," *The New York Times*, 29 July 2012)

THE 45 DWARFS DISNEY REJECTED

Awful. Biggo-Ego. Biggy.
Biggy-Wiggy. Blabby. Busy.
Chesty. Crabby. Cranky.

Daffy. Dippy Dirty.
Dizzy. Doleful. Dumpy.
Flabby. Gabby. Gaspy.

Gloomy. Gloopy. Graceful.
Helpful. Hoppy. Hotsy.
Hungry. Jaunty. Jumpy.

Lazy. Neurtsy. Nifty.
Puffy. Sappy. Scrappy.
Shifty. Silly. Snappy.

Sneezy-Wheezy. Snoopy. Soulful.
Strutty. Tearful. Thrifty.
Weepy. Wistful. Woeful.

(From a book entitled *A Compendium of Indispensable Facts,*
author and date unknown)

HUMILIATION

Body collapsing in on itself
A bowed head
Shoulders curling over chest
Angling torso away from others
Uncontrollable shuddering or shivering
Hair hanging in face, hiding the eyes
A downward gaze
A flushed face
Hitching chest
Eyes dull, lifeless
Pulling down a shirt hem
Hands clutching at stomach
Covering face with hands
Bottom lip or chin trembling
Whimpering
Throat bobbing
Arms falling to sides, lifeless
Uncontrolled tears
Flinching from noise or from being touched
Huddling, crouching
Neck bending forward
Movement is slow, jerky
Knees locked tight together
Cold sweat
Stumbling, staggering
Backing up against a wall
Sliding into a corner
Hiding
Hands gripping elbows
Pigeon toes
Sobs trapped in throat

Drawing knees up to the body's core
Wrapping arms around self
Runny nose

(From *The Emotion Thesaurus: A Writer's Guide to Character Expression* by Angela Ackerman and Becca Puglisi, 2012)

VOICE OF THE MOURNING DOVE

A hollow mournful,
Ooah, cooo, cooo, cooo.

At a distance,
only the three *cooos* are audible.

(From *A Field Guide to the Birds* by Roger Tory Peterson,
Houghton Mifflin, 1947)

NOTHING WILL COME OF NOTHING

We have
looked here

and there
and over there

but didn't
find nothing.

(From "Particle Detector Shows Promise, if Nothing Else" *New York Times*, 4 May 2010)

FOR YOUR REFERENCE

1200 essential words you should know to sound smart
1100 words you need to know

504 absolutely essential words
101 misused words

100 words every high school graduate should know
Word power made easy

(From the titles of vocabulary books in the reference section of
Barnes & Noble)

from *In Short Order*   2018

AUGUST AFTERNOON

The clouds are so white,
so bright, so lit
with the sun's reflection,
so light,
there is nothing
cloudy about them.

A FARM

A farm
without a silo
is like – oh,
I don't know –
a woman
without a man?

THE BEST EVER STUDENT DEFINITION OF POETRY

Poetry is how to
say what cannot be
expressed in words.

ANY POEM BY JOHN ASHBERY

Where poetry goes
when it wants
to be alone.

HIKE

The roots want me to fall down.
The trees want me to stand up to them.

There's a thought.
Now there's a thought.

The stream's days are numbered.
The summer sleeps late.

The past goes it alone
and will soon get lost.

The sky eats my future whole
with my permission.

The sharp rocks kiss the mud.
A frog invents poetry.

KAFKA SAID

Kafka said the most
momentous events of
a person's life occur at
9 am. Yesterday at 9 am
I shaved. Today at 9 am
I took a crap. Tomorrow
at 9 am I'll be teaching
the comma. Damn.
Kafka was right.

MY GARDEN

Tend your garden,
Voltaire said, but
I was a teenager
in the Bronx when
I read *Candide*,
and we didn't have
a garden. I didn't
know what to do,
so I just tended
to my own business
which was staying
off the streets after dark.

NOTHING

Nothing will happen
that has not already happened
to someone else.

The line forms here.

THE GEESE

The geese
on the lake
do not care
how shallow
the bottom is.
They care
how deep
the top is.

THE MOTORCYCLE

The motorcycle
roars down the street
like the wild animal
the rider, entirely
in the skin of a cow,
has always wanted to be.

THE WOMAN

The woman
with the long
legs and no
bra in the café
reading Kafka
aroused my
curiosity.

THOUGHT

I kept the thought
in the back
of my mind
until I confronted it.

WE WERE TALKING

about the worst thing
that could happen to us.
Losing our sight we agreed.
Blindness was the worst thing
that could happen to us.
"I'd get a gun and put
a bullet in my head," I said.
"What a waste," Jim said.
"I'd do a good deed
and marry an ugly woman
to take care of me."

WINNERS AND LOSERS

Of course, they are everywhere
as that is all there are anywhere.

Nature, it seems, has no use
for compromise but has good use

for the compromised.
Just follow the flies.

REQUEST

Please leave
me alone, but

please don't
leave me alone.

AS I SIT IN THE SUN

reading, a butterfly,
a white one, plain
and little, alights on
my arm, grooms itself
for a moment, then flies
off. I put the book down
and close my eyes. "No,
James Wright, I have
not wasted my life.
Life has wasted me."

from *Tomorrow, Today, and Yesterday*   2019

SHORT SPEECH FOR SISYPHUS

See how I torment
my tormentor.
See how I shut him
out of it altogether.
See how I punish myself
by pushing this stone I cut
from this mountain up
this mountain I built.

AFTER THE MOVIE

"See? It didn't end so badly,"
I said. "She didn't die. She
only got married off to that
old man." You didn't say
anything, but the look you
gave me was so deeply cutting,
it severed my balls from the inside.

TOY POEM

This is my toy poem.
I hope you like it.
I made it in the workshop.

I sawed it and sanded it
and glued it and screwed
it and painted it and

finished it to a glossy
finish and signed my
name on the bottom of it.

Please don't pick it up.
Please don't play with it.
It will fall apart.

QUESTION FOR YAHWEH

If, as is said,
you are omnipotent,

and since omnipotence means
that for you all things are possible,

tell me then, why the hell
are you always so damned old?

SONNET OF THE POEM GENOME

Angel, blind bud, calm arrow,
cross curse. Delight dew bride
dream eagle, eternal brow.
Evil evening fate, faith child,

fountain flock fate fox crown.
Gentle, glad glory, grape beast,
grief guest hill. Hell dawn
ivory hawk image, lamb feast

joy. Life lion lord, meadow prayer
melody mercy noble perfume. Passion,
pity, pride, pool purple, shower
rapture, raven robe, rock rose vision.

Sorrow, sorrow soul spirit, storm veil,
wisdom, wandering, weeping sword-soul.

ODE TO THE EAST WIND

Gnieb s'nmutuA fo htaerb uoht,
    dniW tseW dliw O

? dniheb raf eb gnirpS nac,
    semoc retniW fi

, dniw, O! ycehporp a fo
    tepmurt ehT

htrae denekawanu ot spil ym
    hguorht eB

SITTING ON A BENCH

in the park next to a planting
of flowers, trying to think
of nothing, I sneezed. A stranger
passing at that moment said,
"Bless you." I said, "Thank you."
I must have been thinking of nothing.
I really felt blessed. I really was thankful.

NOW

Now that the cherry
tree in front of the house
looks like any other tree,
I will look at all the other trees
with my cherry tree eyes.

IMPROVISATION

When my wife
is out of sorts,

the solution
is at hand.

POETRY

A student came to my office.
"I know what I want to say,
but I don't know how to say it,"
he said. "No problem," I said.
"Read through this for a while,"
I told him as I handed him
a fat anthology of contemporary
American poetry. "You'll learn
how to say it sooner or later."
Another student came to my office.
"I don't know what to say, but
I have this funny feeling that
I already know how to say it,"
he said. "No problem. You're
already a poet," I said as I waved
him out of my office and down
the long, long, dark, dark stairs.

DETOUR

How lost
we are
off the
beaten track.
When we
have to
go back,
how taken aback.

BAD DAY AT THE PIANO

Today you forgot
Chopin's address.

I heard your fingers
running around

the white avenues
and the black

side streets looking
for his house.

CLAIM TO FAME

At the Linden Tree Inn
in Rockport,
Massachusetts,
I sat on
the same toilet seat
that Judy Collins
sat on.

PRESENT

"What do you want for your birthday
this year?" she asked.

"Just get something straight,"
he answered.

DIALOGUE

"You're so predictable,"
she said." You're a cartoon."

"What can I say?
I'm out of my depth," he said.

IN YOSEMITE

In Yosemite,
I left an apple core
at the base of a pine.
I wasn't supposed to.
Neither was the raven
supposed to circle
and circle and circle
and come down to get it.
But I did, and he did.
An apple core at the core
of our twin temptations.
Such partners in crime,
weren't we, Brother Raven?

I'M IN LOVE WITH THE STARBUCKS MERMAID

I'm in love with the Starbucks mermaid.
I'm in love with her Mona Lisa smile.

I'm in love with her eyes of inscrutable green.
Those big green eyes with no pupils.

I'm in love with her long hair of seaweed.
I'm in love with her two fish tails.

How they must wrap you twice around twice.
How they must embrace the very breath out of you.

I adore her crown, toy catamaran with a star for a sail.
Yes, I'm in love with this woman of Lear.

She's the woman who is woman above all adorable.
Yes, I'm in love with her, green and white maid de mer.

Yes, she's the one, she's the one I love.
I'm in love with this fair Melusine.

I'm in love with her.
I'm in love with the Queen of Caffeine.

TEN DOLLARS

I gave ten dollars today to a homeless woman. She was young, in her twenties. She had a dog and a cat. Nine weeks old she said. It was hot. The three of them were sitting on the sidewalk on Fourteenth Street. It was the sunny side of Fourteenth Street. Why she didn't sit on the shady side I don't know. Maybe the money was better on the sunny side. Maybe the passersby were more generous on the sunny side. I don't know. I didn't ask. It was very hot. I gave her ten. I do know this. The wrong people in this world have all the money. I wish I had lots of it, millions and millions. I would give it all to the homeless. I would give it to the girls and the dogs and the cats and the vets of Nam. But it's the wrong people who have the millions and millions. The poets should have all the money. The poets should have the millions and millions. The poets would know what to do with it. The poets wouldn't care what the homeless did with it. There would be no strings attached. Each would pursue happiness in his or her fashion. It would be just as Jefferson said. He, too, was among the wrong people with millions and millions. It's always the wrong people. Walk down the sunny side of Fourteenth Street. You'll see what I mean.

DUNKIN DONUTS

I asked the college kid at
Dunkin Donuts what he
was studying. "Psychology,"
he said. "Okay, why's that?"
I said. "So I can know myself,"
he said. "That's cool," I said.
"A bachelor's in psychology
will certainly help with that,
but do you think, honestly now,
you can make a living knowing
yourself?" "Sure, why not?"
he said. I gave him a $20 tip.

UTILITY

The utility pole
at the bottom
of the driveway
was once a tree
without utility.

from *If You Should See Me Walking on the Road*   2019

IF YOU SHOULD SEE ME WALKING ON THE ROAD

If you should see me walking on the road
alone in the rain, without coat or covering,
my hair matted, the rain running like long
slender plaits of silver hair down my neck
and shoulders, and I am not smiling, do not
be concerned. Do not worry, for I will know
where I am, and I will know where I am going.
But if you should see me walking on the road
alone in the rain, without coat or covering,
my hair matted, the rain running like long
slender plaits of silver hair down my neck
and shoulders, and I am smiling, be concerned.
There will be reason to worry, for I will not know
where I am, and I will not know where I am going.

THE NIGHT IS WARM

The night is warm.
I walk along the lake road.
In the distance, a dog has begun to bark.
It sounds like the slap of a hand against the dark.
In the middle of the lake, the geese stir.
They cry out and shake their wings.
Such a big family.
I envy them that.
It is almost time to settle down for the night.
There is a light at the far end of the lake.
The doctor must be home.
Soon I will be home.
I have very little time.
I must remind myself of everything I know.
There are only two things I know.
Therefore I will not need very much time.
Life has a beginning, a middle, and an end.
Death has a beginning, no middle, and no end.
In the distance the dog has stopped.
The deer must be out of sight.
In the middle of the lake, the geese are quiet.
They have settled down for the night.
At the far end of the lake, the light burns.
The doctor is still awake.
Or he will not be home tonight.

SONG

I have always wanted
(at least ever since
reading Creeley) to
write a poem called
"Song."

Hey, nonny nonny.

MY DOG

So many people with dogs in the park today,
it makes me wonder what kind of dog
I would have if I had a dog. I never had a dog.
When I was five, I was chased by a dog.
I think it was a bull terrier. It looked like the dog
on the old *Our Gang* comedies, but without
the black ring around its eye. It chased me
into the alley behind the apartment building.
I climbed up onto one of the iron bars
that connected the iron railing to the wall.
The dog kept barking as I kept my balance
as best I could, but I was five, and I lost it
and fell off and split my nose open.
Maybe this is why I never had a dog.
There's one I like, a big black one.
The one that looks like a bear.
The one with the big brown doleful eyes.
The one that looks like the only reason
he gets off the couch is to go out to take a crap.
The one whose master is pulling hard on the leash
to get to cross the street into the park.

ADVICE

"Live in the moment,"
my mother told me,
so I lived in the moment.

"Live for the moment,"
my father told me,
so I lived for the moment.

"Live at the moment,"
my grandfather told me,
so I lived at the moment.

"Live around the moment,"
my grandmother told me,
so I lived around the moment.

"Live with the moment,"
my uncle told me,
so I lived with the moment.

"Live about the moment,"
my aunt told me,
so I lived about the moment.

"Live by the moment,"
my girlfriend told me,
so I lived by the moment.

"Live above the moment,"
my teacher told me,
so I lived above the moment.

"Live during the moment,"
my doctor told me,
so I lived during the moment.

"Live along the moment,"
the bartender told me,
so I lived along the moment.

"Live against the moment,"
my lawyer told me,
so I lived against the moment.

I was confused,
so I read a book
by a famous Zen master.

"Live without prepositions,"
he told me,
so I live the moment.

THE WOMAN'S IS THE BETTER BODY

The woman's is the better body.
The man's is the worse.

The woman's body is all four corners of the world.
The man's body is one.

The best the man's body can do
is point to the woman's body.

The most the soul of the man's body can do is say,
"Here is the body I want to be in."

JANUARY

The lake is frozen.
It is ice, and it has snowed, so now
the lake, which is a sheet of ice, is under a blanket of snow.

The wind has died down.
It is still, and the stillness is the ghost of the wind.
Two geese fly over the lake.

Their cries echo against the snow covered ice.
Then they are gone.
Then their cries are gone.

Then the echo is gone.
Then it is still again.
The lake is alone.

TWILIGHT

Twilight and the light follows the sound of a plane west.
The sound fades away, and the light fades after it.
It is pulled, unwilling to leave, and it turns while leaving.
All there is to hear is the water and the birds.

But the sound of the water is not the voice of the water only.
On the tongue of the water is also the voice of the culvert.
And the sound of the birds is not the sound of the birds only.
In the mouths of the birds is also the voice of the empty road.

AFTERGLOW

I asked the poet what her poem
was about because at first I thought
it was about sex, and then I thought it
was about a nuclear war, and then I thought
it was about sex again. I thought it was about
sex because of the lightning and the tides
ebbing and flowing and the crater and,
of course, because of the title, "Afterglow,"
but then I changed my mind and thought
it was about a nuclear war because of
the lightning and the tides ebbing and
flowing and the crater and especially because
the stuff that filled the crater was green
which I took to be new grass growing
after the nuclear war and semen is yellow,
not green, and because of the title, "Afterglow,"
and I changed my mind and thought it was
really about sex after all because of the ending
with its Ah and Oh, aftermath and afterglow,
which so reminded me of the lovely light
of Edna Millay's both-ends-burning candle,
which is about sex. So I asked the poet
what her poem was about, and she stared
at me and said, It's self-evident, and I said,
You're right, I said. It is, I said, How stupid
of me to ask, and she stared at me and said,
That, too, is self-evident and turned away
to talk to someone else, leaving me alone
in the afterglow of the sex of our nuclear war.

ANNIVERSARY

We talked of what years do to us.
It was a fairly average day.
We made love with old, familiar lust.

We put our daughter on the bus.
We said the things we had to say.
We talked of what years do to us.

We had appointments at the dentist,
for cleaning and for x-ray.
We made love with old, familiar lust.

No one called. No one made a fuss.
The January sky was gray.
We talked of what years do to us.

You returned a nightgown, Christmas
gift too big. It was on the way.
We made love with old, familiar lust.

Did we kiss? I think we did kiss.
But anyway... So anyway...
We talked of what years do to us
and made love with old, familiar lust.

APOLOGY TO THE READER

I admit it. I have not written a good
poem. I apologize. There is no excuse.
It should have been good, but it wasn't.
I wrote it the first thing this morning,
before breakfast. That was a mistake.
I have never written a decent poem on
an empty stomach. I shouldn't have tried.
Also, I had to use an unfamiliar pen.
My favorite fine point pen ran out of ink.
I thought I had another in the desk, but
I didn't. I had to resort to a cheap Bic.
The heft was wrong, so it kept slipping
out of my hand. Another thing you should
know. I couldn't find my favorite yellow
legal pad, the one I write good poems on.
I was forced to write on my daughter's spare
sixth grade composition notebook. Even
Robert Frost couldn't write anything
acceptable in that. Anyway, as I said, there's
no excuse for not having written a good
poem. I will make it up to you. I'll write
two good poems tomorrow. After I have
a good breakfast. I promise.

DESK

1.
The desk is a desert.
But where else can I plant
the white flowers?

2.
The desk, the paper, the pen.
These three inseparable brothers.
They even sleep together.

3.
Old man white paper is my guest.
He must not leave without
finishing the black wine.

4.
The desk is getting old.
Every day there are more and more
wrinkles on her face.

5.
The white paper is the door
I have cut in the wall of the desk.
When my pen taps, who will open it to let me in?

6.
The desk is my palomino,
the paper my saddle, the pen my whip.
No, this is cruel.

7.
Tonight the desk
is nothing but my elbows'
hard wooden bed.

HOLY SHIT

Galway Kinnell's "Holy Shit"
is the kind of poem
that gives poetry a bad name.

LAW & ORDER

The only way
to stop

a bad poet
with a pen

is a good poet
with a gun.

from *True Enough*   2019

THE VIRTUE IN VIRTUOSITY IS THE VIRTUE OF THE CITY

The countryside does not make noise.
It lacks the lung power.

It lacks the voice.
The countryside does not draw attention to itself.

It lacks the fluorescent glow.
It lacks the neon glower.

The piano of the countryside is harder to play than the forte of
      the city.
The countryside sings solo.

The countryside sways slow.
The city has no soul,

but the city wants to be soulful,
so the city covers that hole with a lousy virtuoso hollow.

CONGENIALLY CONGENITAL CONJUNCTION

Let us place our bodies together, genitals to genitals.
Let us be friendly and amiable.

Let us do this freely, freely without pressure,
free of obligation, guilt-free, of freedom free, sure to be unsure.

Let us put our bodies close, closer than close,
the closest two bodies can be.

Let them be the most bodies, therefore the least souls.
Let our bodies be all bodies that say, "What are souls?"

Let us put our bodies so close there shall be no space for souls.
Let our souls wander space.

Let our souls leave our bodies and leave our bodies alone.
Bodies are best when left to their own devices.

That's how they devised it.
Let our souls fend for themselves.

Let them find another home away from home.
It will be their loss, poor lost souls.

STUDENT AND ZEN MASTER

"Master, will I ever become Enlightened?"
asked the student.

"Yes, as long as you don't put your mind to it,"
laughed the Master.

I ASKED THE FAMOUS NOVELIST

I asked the famous novelist
if he wrote poetry. "No," he said.
"I'll leave that to you." I nodded
and smiled, but there was something
in his tone I didn't like.
Or the way he held his head.

I FOUND A PENCIL ON THE ROAD

I found a pencil on the road.
It looked like it had been whittled
to expose the lead, not sharpened
with a sharpener. Used for about
two inches of writing. What? Math
homework? Doodles? Poems?
The eraser was rubbed down to gone,
so it must have been poems. I took
it home, wrote this with it, broke it
in half, and threw it out.

I OFTEN WONDER WHAT IT WILL BE LIKE

I often wonder what it would be like,
the morning I do not wake up.
I wonder if it will be like this winter
morning, for instance, the sun shining
brightly enough but cold and distant,
the lake frozen and silent, a desert of ice,
overhead a *v* of geese practicing
to stay in shape while another *v*
follows behind like the other half of
a *w* hurrying to catch up, my neighbor
in a bathrobe going out to the end of
the driveway to get the Sunday paper.
I hope it is but if not, I will understand.
I hope the news is better, but if not,
I will understand.

IN THE PARK NEXT TO THE RIVER

All the butterflies were white.
Then there was a yellow butterfly.

Some of the flowers were yellow.
Some of the flowers were blue.

Some of the flowers were white.
None of the flowers were red.

A sailboat welcomed the wind with open arms.
The wind was white in the sail.

A woman who was tall walked two dogs.
One dog was black.

One dog was white.
A woman who was short walked one dog.

The dog was black and white.
I forgot my guide to the flowers.

I forgot my guide to the butterflies.
I forgot my guide to the sailboats.

I forgot my guide to the wind.
I forgot my guide to the dogs.

I forgot my guide to the women.
I forgot my guide to open arms.

ON THE BRIDGE ABOVE THE RIVER

On the bridge above the river, I had four souls.
They followed the river from north to south.

My first soul was blue, blue from the blue of the sky to the north.
My second soul was green, green from the green of the trees
    along the riverbank.

My third soul was black, black from the shadow of the bridge on
    the river.
My fourth soul was silver, silver from the sun reflected on the
    river to the south.

I had four souls today, one more soul than the river.
It had the blue soul, the green soul, the silver soul, but not the
    black soul.

When I left the bridge, I left three souls with the river.
Only the black soul of the shadow of the bridge did I keep for
    myself.

I keep it close to this day.
It is the only one I have.

SEPHORA

Did Moses' Midianite wife,
Zipporah, really use all this perfume,

all this lipstick,
all this eye shadow,

all this eye liner,
all this lash lengthener,

all this body lotion,
all this face powder,

so much all this that
if I weren't already seventy-two

and thereby have no reason to,
I swear I'd swear off sex?

THAT RED WHEELBARROW

How disappointed I was
when I found out
that the story wasn't true,
that he had noticed it
through the window
of the room of the sick
little girl he was called
to tend to, but that it
actually belonged
to an old black street
vendor in Rutherford.
Of course, so much did
depend on it regardless
of whose it was,
and the rain water
did still glisten on it,
and the white chickens
were still white and
were still going to get
their throats cut. So
perhaps it's a good thing
it was the street vendor's.
The little girl would
have given them names.

THE CHILDREN

are playing in the schoolyard.
Some are running.

Some are skipping.
Some are swinging.

Some are kicking a ball.
Some are tossing a disk.

Two are flying.
I am a child.

I am not running.
I am not skipping.

I am not swinging.
I am not kicking a ball.

I am not tossing a disk.
I am flying, flying, flying.

THE LAKE IS A GOOD LISTENER

The lake is a good listener.
It has an open mind.
It listens to the wind without turning away.
It listens to the trees without yawning.
It listens to the frogs without laughing in their faces.
It listens to the geese without mimicking them.
It even listens to me, I, who have so much less to say
than the geese, than the frogs, than the trees, than the wind,
without shaking its head and mumbling under its breath.

THE THREE-MONTH OLD

The three-month old
in the stroller was staring at me.
What was she thinking?
I tell you honestly,
I would pay her college tuition
to know what was in her three-month old
mind while she was staring at me.

ASHES TO ASHES

Jim's brother died last week. We went
to the funeral home to pick up the ashes.
"Why is it called a funeral home?" I said.
"Is it the home of fuckin funerals?"
"Could be. Maybe because it's more
like our home away from home," Jim said.
"It's heavy," said the funeral director
handing Jim a shopping bag with the box
with the ashes with his brother without a home.
"He ain't heavy," Jim said. "He's my brother."
The funeral director didn't laugh. "Animals
don't go to funeral homes when they die,"
I said. "Shit, why do we?" "Right," Jim said.
"The whole fuckin earth is their home."
"So what are you going to do with Mike's ashes?"
I said. "Spill them somewhere nice," Jim said.
"Around here? I thought he didn't come from
around here," I said. "Maybe I should send
it up to his wife in New Hampshire. She
ought to decide what to do," Jim said.
"I guess so," I said. "But you have the ashes.
Don't you think you ought to decide what
to do with them?" "Maybe. After all, I did
know him longer than his wife did," Jim said.
"Let's go find some place nice." "That place
on the Delaware?" I said. "Yeah," Jim said.
"Where we saw the three girls in the raft
take off their tops and wave at us?" I said.
"Yeah, that's the one," Jim said. "That place."

I WENT TO THE LIBRARY

I went to the library
to give my two new books
to Matt, the head librarian,
to put on the shelf. "Hey,
Matt," I said. "Here are my
latest books to put on the poetry
shelf." (It's a small library.
It has only one poetry shelf.)
"Well, you know, I have
to review them," he said.
"Okay," I said. "You have
three of my books already,
so just read them and put
them on the shelf next to
those." "Well," he said,
"there's very little space."
(Matt says "well" a lot.)
"Okay," I said. "But, you
know, they're really thin
books. They're poetry. Like
the other three. Just squeeze
them in, okay?" (I say "okay"
a lot.) I think he smiled. "I'll
review them," he said. "Oh,
one more thing," I said. "You
spelled my name wrong."
I handed him the page in
the catalogue I printed out
for one of my books. Next
to author was "Salanche, J.R."
"Oh, yeah, I see," Matt said.
"That's tough. I'll have to delete
the whole thing and enter it

from scratch all over again."
He shook his head. I think
he smiled again. Or he could
have been smiling the whole
time. "Okay," I said. "Thanks."
So much for immortality.

KOOSER

Ted, you say your
poem about your dead
parents is dark. I say
you do darkness with
a light touch, so the rest
of us may see better in it.

A COLLEAGUE AND I WERE TALKING

A colleague and I were talking
in the hall between classes. "I just
read that most men think about sex
more than anything else," she said.
"I guess I'm not most men because
I don't think about sex more than
anything else," I said. "No?" she said.
"No," I said. "Well, what do you think
about more than anything else?" she said.
"I think about poetry more than anything
else," I said. "Oh," she said. "I get it.
You think about something you can actually
do something about." "That's right," I said.
"You know, that's right," I said again.

from *In a Public Place*   2019

HOW THE ERIE LEFT TOWN

The crossing-gates
went first,
and with them
the flashing red signal lights.

Then the tracks,
after a century
bolted to the earth,
were gone.

And the oak ties,
black as soot,
were taken,
and the spikes

like rusted carrots
were gone,
pulled up,
harvested for scrap.

Finally, the air
left town,
heavy with a
hundred years of bells.

PARKING LOT POEM

So here I am in the parking
lot of the shopping mall,
the fourth best place to write
a poem, after the garret in
the hotel on Montmartre,
after the round tower
of the medieval castle on
the Irish coast, after any prison
cell anywhere. It is a big
parking lot, and the sky over
it is a big sky, big as a continent
with its own mountains and
cities and rivers and plains
of cloudy wheat. The sky
is bigger than the sky you
would see from the garret,
from the tower, from
any prison cell anywhere.

SATURDAY

On the street in town,
everyone is carrying something,
everyone's arms are full.

This old man is carrying
fifty years of newspapers.
Each year is a bundle tied in string.

His back is bent from the weight.
This wife is carrying her past.
It is made of glass. It is extremely fragile.

She carries it in a velvet pouch
inside a wooden box inside a metal case
inside a leather satchel with two straps.

The husband is carrying Monday.
He holds it like a dozen roses.
He holds it like the wheel of a fast car.

This teenaged boy is carrying three futures.
They are light as feathers, as bubbles.
He tosses them up before him as he walks.

This old woman is carrying death.
She holds it in her arms like a newborn.
She is singing it a lullaby under her breath.

I am carrying myself on a tray.
I am a waiter delivering the meal.
Arrogant and aloof, I balance myself

on my right hand, over the heads
of the others. My left arm swings freely.
It clears my way to your table.

SHADE GARDEN

I asked the gardener working
in the shade garden what
he was doing. He said
he was pruning the shade.
Shade grows fast in the
afternoon and must be cut
back or it will encroach
on the sun, which is also
grown in the shade garden.
I asked him if shade is a
difficult plant to grow.
He said it needs full sun
and constant maintenance.
It is always changing size
and shape and it is difficult
to keep up with. I could
see how tired he was from
a long day's work, so
I thanked him and went on
my way to the rose garden,
which was almost risen.

WEST 64th STREET

I saw it at the end of the block,
homeless against the shins
of the apartment building,
bundled in old cord. I crossed
the street and ran my hand
over the strings of the harp,
and ran my hand over
the strings of the harp, and
I ran my hands over the strings
and over the strings, and I saw
the pain of the world, all
the pain of the world, fly up
into the air over West 64th
Street, up into the air and up, up
into the dark, dark sky.

BROOKLYN BRIDGE

How much smaller it looks in stone
and steel than in its photographs.

Even the least of buildings tower over it.
But it was here first.

It is like the old cemeteries cities let lie.
Like the ones they fence off, and surround

with the new because the prominent are buried there.
There is something of the grave about it.

There is the somber dark of the stones.
There is the skeleton of the cables ossified against the sky.

AMERICA

I sit on a bench in front
of the Department of Justice,
under the massive magnolia
tree, thinking about the meaning
of justice, when the metallic
smell of the homeless man
across the avenue mingles with
the aroma of the magnolia flowers.
Such a strange perfume they make.
Let us call it *America*.

VIETNAM WAR MEMORIAL

It is a laceration in
the earth where napalm
has fallen and burned it to char.

It is an unclosing wound
enclosing us in our mass
grave, slowly, so slowly.

It is the lipstick stain
of this war's
black kiss.

A COUPLE IS FRENCH KISSING

A couple is French kissing
on a bench in Washington
Square Park. Everyone is
looking, including me.
After a long time, she opens
her eyes and looks my way
over his shoulder. She
has beautiful blue eyes.
I smile. She smiles. They
get up, she tosses her light
brown hair, they walk arm
in arm toward the Bobst
Memorial Library whose
ceiling Galway Kinnell
wrote a poem about with
the last line, *I do not want*
to die, I want to be born.
No, no, we do not want to die.
Yes, yes, we want to be born.

IN A PUBLIC PLACE

i
The flag flutters.
The white and pink petals fall.
One breeze is enough.

ii
Piped into the men's room,
a Beethoven string quartet.
I wish I were constipated.

iii
On another bench,
a man reads a book of poetry.
Someday I want to write

a book of poetry
that cannot be read in public.
It will be illegal.

iv
The flowering plant is doing its job:
being publicly private,
being privately public.

v
The material dematerializes.
One deity dies.
Another is born.

vi
Look! The moon is made of money.
Let us spend it on happiness.
It will be sold out soon.

from *To Say the Least*   2019

BROTHER WREN

Brother Wren,
when I hear you sing,
I wish I were you
so I could mind my
own business
without questioning
what my business is,
or what my mind is,
or what my *is* is.
Every little thing
without questioning.

NOT ENOUGH IS NOT ENOUGH

We did not know how many were enough.
Therefore we did not know when to stop.
Therefore we did not stop.
We did not know what we were talking about.
Therefore you continued to talk about stars.
Therefore I continued to talk about wounds.
Therefore we did not stop.
That is how it happened.
That is how the stars got to be wounds.
That is how the wounds got to be stars.

GAIA

She does not experiment.
She is not a scientist.
She is not a clinician.
She is not a sociologist.
She is not a psychologist.
She says everything once.
She never repeats herself.
She throws you in the deep end.
Sink or swim.
Swim for your life.

HOW TO SIT

Always make sure
there's an empty chair
next to you for the one
who has nothing on his
mind, so you can learn how
he attained enlightenment.

ON EDGE

I was on edge
all day, but even so,
even after many tries,
I still could not get
a word in edgewise.

THE DUKE OF ALL DAY

Play man Play
While I Work
While you Make
My work Play

Work man Work
Let the German Wait
For my Mood
To swing Back

Again his Way
Play man Play
If it ain't Got
That Wenden

You know What
It don't Mean

LOST AND FOUND

It's usually the other
way around

isn't it?
Found and lost?

Or did I misunderstand?
Is it "found out"

and "lost out"
that I was thinking about?

ON THOUGHT'S TERMS

Here I am,
in terms
of thought.

O, GENERAL

O, general, the rockets.
O, general, the bombs.

O, general, the woman buried alive.
O, general, the child burned but alive.

O, general, "A war to the death," you say.
O. general, what war is not a war to the death?

O, general, logic plus logic equals insanity.
O, general, the world is the saddest place on earth.

HEARING TEST

The hearing test says I'm losing it.
The higher frequencies are less frequent.

The top register doesn't register.
So goodbye tree frogs.

Goodbye crickets.
Goodbye birds of the high pitches.

Goodbye sopranos.
Goodbye falsettos.

Goodbye piccolo and flute.
Goodbye squeals of playground delight.

Goodbye.
Goodbye.

Goodbye.

THE DEATH OF MY SHADOW

I watch my shadow
cross the street.

I watch the shadow of the taxi
run down my shadow crossing the street.

I watch the shadow of the taxi driver
get out of the shadow of the taxi

and curse my shadow
as it lies dying in the street.

I watch the shadow of the ambulance
carry my shadow to the shadow

of the hospital where my shadow
never regains consciousness,

where it dies of internal injuries.
I watch the funeral of my shadow.

I watch the shadow of the rabbi,
the shadows of my relatives,

your shadow, a widow's shadow,
beautiful in black, mourning my shadow.

ONE WORD

One word leads
to another,

and someday,
perhaps,

I'll discover
exactly

what that
word is.

from *The Porch Poems*   2020

THERE'S SOMETHING TO BE SAID

There's something
to be said
for a place
where the tallest
building is a church.

SMALL PLEASURES

What a pleasurable
perversity it is to sit
in the rocking chair
without rocking it.

I MET A YOUNG MAN

I met a young man
today who said he named
his cat Socrates. He was
about twenty or so. I told him
about the philosopher
after whom he named his cat,
and ancient Athens, and
how he was accused of
corrupting the youth of Athens,
twenty-somethings like himself,
and how he was found guilty
and sentenced to death
and how he drank hemlock
and died. He didn't know
what I was talking about,
so I asked him why he
named his cat Socrates,
and he said it was a cool
name, and I had to agree.
It was a cool name.

THE FLOWERS AT NIGHT

The flowers at night are all the same.
And at night, the trees are all the same.
So, too, are the clouds at night the same.
Only the wind at night is different,
so different as it moans its secrets
to the unwilling who cannot turn away.

WHEN I SAW IT ON THE GROUND

When I saw it on the ground,
struggling to get up,
the yellow wings beating so hard
against the earth I swear I could hear them,
I said a little prayer,
and in a heart-beat,
we both were blessed with what we wanted.
For me, it was the only prayer ever answered.
For the monarch, it was the only ever sky.

MONOSYLLABIC

The best ones are the small ones,
those you need to hold in your hand
two or three at a time, those you need
to feel for size, and shape, and heft,
the blunt, the sharp, the smooth,
the rough, the square, the round,
the firm, the soft, the ones like rocks,
like bricks or stones in streams,
the ones like clods of soil or clumps
of clay, the ones you pile to build
the whole world with, and then
the ones you hurl to bring it down.

THIRTY-TWO ONE-LINERS ON DEATH

Death doesn't have a face, for it is just a mouth the exact same shape as your mind.

Death doesn't have a body, for it is just ten fingers, each the exact same size as your body.

Death doesn't have a mind, for it uses yours.

Death is funny sometimes, for it comes when you most expect it.

For many, death is the best thing ever to happen to life.

Before we are born we are not alive, yet we do not call this death.

Death is the second greatest mystery in life.

The opposite of death is not life; it is sex..

Death brings us full circle, but circles do not exist.

Death is what we wish upon our enemies when imagination fails us.

To the question, "Death, where is thy sting?" the answer is, "In the left anterior descending coronary artery."

The reason why we meet death with such astonishment is we have no memory of being born.

Death has a generous spirit, for it allows us to believe anything, right up to the very end.

Death is a dead end without end.

Death is the life of the party.

Indifference to life is only possible when we are first indifferent to death.

Death may be on the other side of life, but it is still on this side of the Great Mystery.

Death is in the details.

Death is our preoccupation until it is our post-occupation.

Death has a heart of lead which philosophers have for centuries sought to transmute into gold in vain.

Death answers everyone but answers to no one.

Life's blood is death's life's blood.

Of all the millions who live vicarious lives, not one, not a single solitary one, ever dies a vicarious death.

Death makes strange bedfellows.

Feel sorry for Death; he can never have the last laugh.

All death is local.

At the time of our death, everything falls into place.

I'm not afraid of death; I just hate its guts.

Feel sorry for death; it doesn't have a life its own.

Death is the last fact of life.

Have a heart, Death!

Alas, death doesn't hear us; death is dead to the world.

PROSPERO

So every third thought
shall be the grave. But
what shall every first
thought be, and every
second thought? A blow-
job? A glass of wine?
His grandchild on his
knee? A nap in the sun?
Or as Dustin Hoffman
said about retirement,
a good baked potato
and a good crap?

MISTAKE

Odd word, *mistake*.
It means an error
caused by a lack of skill.
Just think.
A life, a whole life,
can be an error
caused by a lack of skill.

TO MY LEFT HAND

Yes, little brother, I see you.
Yes, you want attention.
You're holding my chin in place.
You're massaging my nose.
You're tugging at my left earlobe.
And, no, I will not forget.
You're the one who jerks me off.
While it's big brother who jerks
me off the other way.
The public way. This way.
Yes, I hear you, little brother.
You're the one who snaps
in time to the blues
on the radio. Or slaps my thigh.
You're the one who drums
on the desk. The one who
wears the ring and reminds me
thereby of my responsibilities.
And, no, I will not forget
my promise that when both
of you are sleeping on
my sleeping chest,
you will be the one on top.

ON THE BIRTHDAY OF JOHN KEATS

On the birthday of John Keats,
I wanted to write a poem
for his birthday, something
formal, a sonnet or an ode,
something with stanzas,
iambic meter and rhyme,
you know, something in his style.
Unfortunately, I haven't been
able to do much of what I
want these days. For instance,
this morning I wanted
to make love to my wife.
We went for a walk instead.

I HEARD A BIRD

I heard a bird.
I think it was a mourning dove.
I got up to see what it was.
It wasn't there.
I heard a cricket.
When I looked for it, I couldn't find it.
I heard rustling in the grass.
I investigated and found nothing.
I heard a whirring.
I walked around the house.
I didn't see anything.
I heard laughter in the wild cherry tree.
I didn't get up.
I knew what it was.
I joined them in their laughter at me.

NOTHING GHAZAL

When writing a ghazal, you can't go wrong to quote the Masters,
such as "Full of sound and fury signifying nothing."

Or this one, also by Master Shakespeare:
"Nothing will come of nothing."

Speaking of Shakespeare, he wrote some really funny plays.
My favorite funny play is *Much Ado about Nothing.*

Here's a nice example by the brothers Gershwin,
Master George and Master Ira, "I've got plenty of nothing."

And here's one by the Irish master, Samuel Beckett:
"Where you have nothing, there you should want nothing."

This might be the best, from Master Plato's *The Republic:*
"I am the wisest man alive, for I know one thing, and that is that
     I know nothing."

So, Solonche, why not quote Master Bukowski to end this thing?
"It was good in there, nothing ever occurred in there, no people,
     nothing."

EMILY DICKINSON'S DOG

Emily Dickinson's dog
was a Newfoundland.
His name was Carlo.
What a wonderful name.
She certainly had a flair
for the exotic, didn't she?
But Carlo is nowhere
to be found in the poems.
The name I mean. Even
in the famous one in which
she leaves early and takes
her dog, she doesn't name
him. Why didn't she
immortalize Carlo, I wonder,
the way Christopher Smart
immortalized his cat,
Jeoffry? No, there's no
Carlo in all of Dickinson.
I know. I checked the index
to her *Complete Poems*.
But if she had written one,
I bet it would have begun
something like this,
"I'm Carlo – Who are You?"
He lived to be 16,
a ripe old age for a large
breed of dog. And when he died,
she grieved. She grieved for a long, long time.

MY NEIGHBOR

is hammering
what has to be
a very big nail
into a very thick
hunk of wood.
Either that or
he is fantasizing
killing his wife.

GOING BACK TO THE BULLSHIT SHIT-ASS WAR

He was a student wounded in Fallujah in Iraq.
He was absent a lot, and he never spoke in class.
He came by to tell me he was going back.

I asked him, "What the hell you doing that for, Mike?"
He said he knew. He knew it was a bullshit shit-ass
war, this student wounded in Fallujah in Iraq.

He smiled and stopped smiling. He said, "Fuck
this war. Shit, the army pays tuition. Books. Gas."
He just dropped by to say that he was going back.

I stared at his t-shirt, which was entirely black
with white letters, a rock band called *Critical Mass*.
This was my student wounded in Fallujah in Iraq.

"I understand," I said. "But you may not have such luck
next time." "Yeah," he said. "But this too shall pass."
He shrugged and said that anyway he was going back.

"I really think that you should get your life on track,"
I said. He stood up, saluted and left the office.
That was it, a student wounded in Fallujah in Iraq
who had just stopped by to tell me he was going back.

THE EMPTY STOOL

She was tall and proud and beautiful.
Her glasses were dark, and her hair was red.
She strode to the bar and took the center stool.

It was love at first sight, at second, and hell,
at third as she smiled and turned her head.
God, she was tall and smart and beautiful.

I lifted, tilted my dark brown Scottish ale.
She tilted, sweetly lifted beer "Hop Dread."
So I moved one stool closer to her center stool.

We talked about books, history, the modern novel,
and *Beowulf,* which she meant to but had never read.
O, but she was tall and witty and beautiful.

"I recommend Heaney's. It's wonderful."
I leaned a little toward her ear as I whispered.
But she moved one stool over from my closer stool.

She stood. Before she left me there an utter fool,
she shook my hand. "Nice meeting you," she said.
O, yes, she was tall and cold and beautiful,
and her fingers, the steel of the empty stool.

I WANT A FIREMAN'S FUNERAL

I want a fireman's funeral when I die.
I want to be sent off by the older generation
of firemen and the younger generation of firemen.
I want the flag at the firehouse to fly at half-staff.
I want the black and purple funereal bunting to be draped
over the big doors of the brick firehouse.
I want flowers on the pumper at the head of the procession,
white lilies and yellow lilies and red carnations,
all resting on a bed of long green ferns.
I want my black rubber fireman's boots standing reversed
next to the other boots not reversed on the back of the pumper.
I want the fire trucks following the pumper polished
and gleaming, their red lights flashing silently,
the hook and ladder, the rescue vehicle, the chief's car.
I want all the brass polished and gleaming in the sunlight.
I want all the chrome polished and gleaming almost
to blinding in the sunlight.
I want the mascot, the Dalmatian, sitting in the pumper
next to the driver acknowledging the people along
the route of the procession.
He will miss the morning scratch behind the ears I gave him.
I want the older generation of firemen in their just
washed cars following the fire trucks,
trailing drops of water on the road.
I want the younger generation of firemen in their just
washed cars following them,
trailing drops of water on the road.
Had I known how stately and ceremoniously beautiful
is a fireman's funeral,
I would have become one.
But I did not know, and I did not become one,
and I feel sorry for myself,
for I will not have a fireman's funeral when I die.

from *For All I Know*   2020

POETRY

"I like your poem," I told the student.
"It's really good." "Thanks," she said.
"You should publish more," I said.
"I don't have any more right now,"
she said. "I'm very hard on myself."
"That's good," I said. "Being hard on
yourself is the best way to be. It will
make things a lot easier later on.
You'll see." I'm such a fucking liar.
Not about the poem. The poem really
was good. About the later on part.

THE FEMINIST POET

Don't you see her red tongue wag?
Isn't it just like lewd laundry?

And her nipples, aren't they like the tips of ballpoint pens?
Don't you get bitten by the zipper of her lines?

Doesn't your mind catch and run?
Don't you, too, want to run?

A MAN SITS IN A WORLD OF SUNSHINE AND LILIES

A man sits in a world of sunshine and lilies.
A newspaper is in his lap.
In the newspaper is a world of smoke and blood.
He does not know which one is real.
A woman sits in the world of smoke and blood.
No newspaper is in her lap.
There is no world of sunshine and lilies for her to see.
She needs not wonder which one is real.
She knows the world of smoke and blood is real.
She knows the smoke is real.
It is in her lungs.
She knows the blood is real.
It is on her hands.
She knows her scream is real.
It is the voices of her mother and her mother's mother.
It is her voice three times over.
She knows her pain is real.
It tastes of her own heart.
She knows any other world is not real.
She knows any other world is a dream.
She knows there is no such thing as a dream.
She knows there is no such place as a world of sunshine and
          lilies.
The lilies turn black in his lungs.
The sunshine turns red on his hands.

HAIKU FOR SOLO PIANO

The pianist in black
comes out, shakes hands with the piano.
They are attending the same funeral.

"The Steinway is dead,"
he said. "Wheel out the Yamaha
ha ha ha instead."

"The coffin of music,"
quipped James Joyce.
But listen, listen in living black and white.

The intermission:
Silent piano silent movie.
Unaccompanied.

The pianist in black
comes out, shakes hands with the piano.
They are going to play championship chess.

The huge black mouth,
nearly the size of the summer night.
"Listen," it says. "Here is a dream even longer than yours."

SHORT SPEECH FOR ADAM

When I woke up
from that deep sleep,
I saw her there,
standing a few yards
away, in the shade
of two trees, with her
hands on her hips,
speaking to me in
the language of the hyenas.

THE BOOK OF LILAC

I have an idea for a book.
It will be a book of poems
about the lilac tree in my front
yard. Every poem in it will be
about the tree, and there will be
a hundred of them. I have the title.
It will be called *The Book of Lilac.*
Of course, I will never write such
a book, a book of a hundred poems
about the lilac in my front yard.
But I have written five or six,
so maybe with a little luck,
I won't have to write it to be
remembered for having written it.
Maybe with a little luck, someone
a hundred years from now will
come across these five or six poems
about a lilac tree in my front yard
and remember a vague reference
to a book entitled *The Book of Lilac*
and believe those five or six poems
were the only ones not lost in
the same dust in the same corner
of the same cellar of all lost books
of poetry. It is possible, with a little luck.

THE DAY BEFORE

The day before
the swamp freezes
over, the black water
seizes the sun
and pulls it under.

TWO OLD INDIANS

"They sound like
chattering crows,
don't they?" said one.
"Yeah, but I understand
crows. I don't understand
that tribe," the other said.

FIRE

"When one burns one's bridges, what a very nice fire
it makes," is a great quote by the Welsh poet Dylan Thomas.

"Just as a candle cannot burn without fire,
men cannot live without a spiritual life," said the Buddha.

"Education is not the filling of a pail, but the lighting of a fire."
This was said by the Irish poet William Butler Yeats.

John Wesley, founder of Methodism, said, "Catch on fire
and people will come for miles to see you burn."

Earth is the only known planet with fire.
There isn't enough oxygen anywhere else.

Written in 1938, "I Don't Want to Set the World on Fire"
is a pop song recorded most notably by The Ink Spots.

So, Solonche, aren't you going to fix the format of this
        ghazal on fire?
Yes. Here goes. Stand back. *Ready fire. Aim fire. Fire fire.*

STONE

He's not my savior, but I like a lot of things Jesus said.
One is, "Let him who is without sin cast the first stone."

I never thought I'd quote Keith Richards (even use his name in a
     poem),
but "you've got the sun, you've got the moon, and you've got the
     Rolling Stones."

"I know not with what weapons World War III will be fought,"
     said Albert Einstein
more seriously, "but World War IV will be fought with sticks and
     stones."

"Stoned" is borrowed from older expressions like "stone drunk"
     or "stone cold."
This is consistent with the now familiar image of the supine life
     less "stoner."

In England in 1389 a royal statute fixed the standard unit of
     wool at 14 pounds.
It is still used for people and large animals and is called a
     "stone."

There are many forms of inhumane execution in the world.
The most barbaric is from the Bible, death by stoning.

So, Solonche, any last words to share with us about this
     interesting word?
Carve *He cast a cold eye on life, on death but with a twinkle in it*
     on my headstone.

SUN

Because he died by refusing to breathe, Diogenes is my favorite
     philosopher.
He famously told Alexander not to stand between him and the sun.

He also said, "The sun, too, shines into cesspools and is not
     polluted."
The closest thing to a perfect sphere so far observed is the sun.

Osiris, Apollo, and Balder are all personifications of the sun.
Jonah, Cain, and Noah are all related to the rising and resting of
     the sun.

The Japanese flag is the rising sun.
Namibia, Argentina, Uruguay, Bangladesh, Taiwan, Rwanda all
     show the sun.

A hit song by The Beatles from 1969 is "Here Comes the Sun."
A hit song by The Doors from 1968 is "Waiting for the Sun."

A hit song by Lou Reed (sorry, no year) is "Ride into the Sun."
My favorite, by The Animals from 1964, is "The House of the
     Rising Sun."

So, Solonche, got one more of these before we're done?
I was born under the moon, but I wish to die in the sun.

DREAM

The word "dream" comes from the Middle English word
    "dreme."
My favorite Shakespeare comedy is *A Midsummer Night's
    Dream.*

The structure of the atom came to Niels Bohr in a dream.
The structure of the benzene molecule came to August Kekulé in
    a dream.

The Theory of Relativity came to Einstein after a vivid dream.
Mendeleev arranged the table of the 63 known (1869) elements
    in a dream.

Mary Shelley's famous novel *Frankenstein* was inspired by a
    dream.
The plot of *Dr. Jekyll and Mr. Hyde* came to R.L. Stevenson in an
    opium dream.

The famous poem "Kubla Khan" came to S.T. Coleridge in an
    opium dream.
An influential book (1899) by Sigmund Freud is *The Interprettion
    of Dreams.*

Carl Jung (1875 – 1960) broke with Freud over their differing
    views on dreams.
Edgar Allan Poe said, "All that we see or seem, is but a dream
    within a dream."

So, Solonche, la la la la la la la la la la la la life is but a dream?
I hope life is but a dream because if it is then death too is but a
    dream.

WORD

The word *word* comes from Old English and from the Proto-
    Gemanic *wurda*.
Chinese proverb: "If you wish to know the mind of a man, listen
    to his words."

Confucius: "A gentleman would be ashamed should his deeds not
    match his words."
Pythagoras: "Silence is better than unmeaning words."

Moliere: "I live on good soup, not on fine words."
Ludwig van Beethoven: "Music comes to me more readily than
    words."

Mauve is Nabakov's favorite word.
Edith Piaf: "I want to make people cry even when they don't
    understand my words."

A four letter word is another name for a swear word.
A saying used all the time is, "A picture is worth a thousand
    words."

Hamlet: (*The Tragedy of Hamlet, Prince of Denmark* II, ii, 210)
    "Words, words, words."
One of my students: "Poetry expresses what we cannot say in
    words."

So, Solonche, tell us, what's the good word?
I couldn't tell you, so I'd rather let this ghazal have the last word.

APPLE

From Middle English *appel*, from Old English *æppel* from
  Proto-Germanic *aplaz*.

The very first word Emily, our daughter we adopted from China,
  spoke was "apple."

The fruit of the Tree of Knowledge was a pomegranate not an
  apple.
This means Steve Jobs should have called his company
  Pomegranate instead of Apple.

Grown around the world are over 7,500 varieties of apples.
The only apple native to the United States is the crabapple.

Johnny Appleseed planted apple trees for hard cider, not for
  eating apples.
Malusdomesticaphobia is the fear of apples.

A trench mortar used by the British in World War I was the
  "Toffee Apple."
For two days I worked at an orchard picking (on a fucking 20
  foot ladder!) apples.

New York City (or only Manhattan) is also known as "The Big
  Apple."
At New York University, I knew a girl from Montreal, Canada,
  named Pomey.

So, Solonche, how do you like them apples?
I like all them apples, but the only one I ever loved is the last
  apple.

DANCE

Middle English: from Old French *dancer* (verb), *dance* (noun), of
    unknown origin.
Terpsichore (the most beautiful of the nine) is the Greek Muse of
    dance.

As I promised, now I can quote the correct idiom of a song and a
    dance.
I never went to my high school prom because I didn't know how
    to dance.

One of the biggest hit songs (The Bee Gees) is "You Should Be
    Dancing."
The debut (2008) single (Grammy nominated 2009) by Lady
    Gaga was "Just Dance."

The samba of Brazil is the world's most popular folk dance.
Baladi is a form of Egyptian belly dance, a truly hypnotic dance.

The hora is a popular Israeli circle dance.
Popular in South Africa is the gumboot (they wear Wellingtons)
    dance.

Clogging is the official Kentucky and North Carolina state dance.
Minnesota is the only state that has no official state dance.

So, Solonche, will you, won't you, will you, won't you, won't you
    join the dance?
Oh, someday, one day, maybe Sunday, I may, I mean, I might
    join the dance.

THE WIND

The sky is broken into clouds.
The clouds are broken into the children of themselves.

The twigs have broken from the branches.
The leaves have broken from the twigs.

The earth is the heart of the sky, and it is breaking.
The world breaks every promise it makes.

It has never been taught to keep them.
Every promise is broken twice, once before and once after.

The earth never breaks its promises.
You can always tell where the wind has been.

It tells you with the song it learns there.
The wind minds its manners.

It knocks – one, two, three times – before it enters your house.
Of all the animals, the wind loves the horses the most.

Of all the birds, the falcon it has yet to conquer.
The stems of the lilies have been broken in half.

The heads of the lilies have been broken off.
The petals of the lilies have been broken away.

The wind is not afraid of the dark.
The wind makes its own way in the world.

The wind whistles while it works.
The wind takes your breath away, then breaks it.

Trying to get out, the wind has broken its neck against the wall at the end of the world.

LINDA'S OFFICE SUPPLY

I was in Linda's Office Supply.
She was laminating a poem for me.
Never mind why.
That's another story.

A woman came in.
She wanted to buy a scent-free candle.
Linda showed the woman a scent-free candle.
The woman wanted to buy matches.

Linda didn't have matches.
Neither did I.
Linda gave me my laminated poem.
I paid and left.

I was wrong.
It's the same story, not another story.
Linda made nine copies of "Beer Ghazal."
I leave them in the bars I go to with Jim on Saturdays.

I'll be going back to Linda's Office supply for more.
The lamination protects them from beer spills as well as tear
        spills.
Poems must be beer-proof.
Poems must be tear-proof, especially, especially.

I don't know why the woman needed a scent-free candle and
        matches.
It must have been important whatever it was.
It is the only story we know.
It is the story that involves tears.

O blessings upon you.
O blessings upon whatever it was.
O blessings upon blessings upon blessings upon you.
O Woman with Scent-free Candle Burning, Burning that No
      Tears May Extinguish!

CUTTY SARK

The jazz musician in the movie drank Cutty Sark.
I'm a sucker for jazz music.
I'm a sucker for movies about jazz musicians.
Weel done, Cutty-sark!
And in an instant all was dark.

I'm a sucker for jazz musicians who drink Scotch.
This one drank a bottle every night.
I'm a sucker for a jazz musician who does that and still makes
    music.
Weel done, Cutty Sark!
And in an instant all was dark.

I wanted to see if I could drink and still make poems.
I found out that I could not.
I found out that I could not drink and still make poems.
Weel done, Cutty-sark!
And in an instant all was dark.

I found out that I wasn't cut out to be maker of poems.
It has taken my whole life.
It has taken my whole life to find out I'm not cut out to make
    poems.
Weel done, Cutty-sark!
And in an instant all was dark.

But it's not too late.
It's not too late to learn to make a poem.
There is still time, still time, still time.
Weel done, Cutty-sark!
And in an instant all was dark.

There is still time, still time, still time.
There is yet time to make a poem, to make but one.
There is still time to be a poet once for all who makes a perfect
       rhyme.
Weel done, Cutty-sark!
And in an instant all was dark.

from *Enjoy Yourself*   2020

HOME

We are so adaptable,
so amazingly adaptable,

that no matter where
we find ourselves,

we manage to make
ourselves at home,

even at home,
even there.

A SMALL CLOUD

A small cloud drifts overhead.
The cloud is actually eight small clouds.
It is an island chain of clouds.
Soon it evaporates.
Soon it disappears.
I must remember this when I am asked,
"What is the soul?"

THE BARE MAXIMUM

At most,
it is
the least
you can do.

TESTIMONY

I want to testify.
I want to give an opening statement.
I want to answer questions for the record.
I want to place my left hand on the Bible even though I don't
     believe in it.
I want to raise my right hand.
I want to swear to tell the truth.
I want to swear to tell the whole truth.
I want to swear to tell nothing but the truth.
I want to swear so help me god even though I don't believe in it.
I want to do this officially in the presence of officials.
I want to prove a poet can tell the truth.
I want to prove a poet can tell the whole truth.
I want to prove a poet can tell nothing but the truth.
I want to prove a poet can do this without telling it slant.
I want to tell what I saw.
I want to tell what I heard.
I want to tell what I know for sure.
I want the bastard to go to prison for life without parole.
I want the motherfucker to die in prison because I put him there.

MERRIMENT

I laughed to myself
when I heard them
laugh out loud about
a secret joke until, out
of ear shot, I laughed out
loud at my secret joke
louder than they laughed.

A HOUSE

Is a house a home?
Is a home sweet?
Is a home where you hang your hat?
If a house is not a home, what is?
Can a room be a home?
Can a room in a house that is not a house be a home?
Is it a heart?
The heart can be a home to many things.
The heart can be a home to many belongings.
But the heart can be a home to only one long longing.
The heart can be the home to one long longing that never leaves.
Is the lady of the house at home?
Is the man of the house at home?
Is the lady of the house wearing a blue blouse?
Is the man of the house a louse?
Is the lady of the house his spouse?
Is the man of the house her spouse?
Is the lady of the house chasing a mouse?
Is the man of the house a souse?
Is the lady of the house wearing no blouse?
Does the man of the house do nothing all day but grouse?
The heart is the house where the one long longing that never
      leaves is at home.
The heart is the world's most expensive house.
The heart is the world's smallest house.

I JUST READ AN AWFUL POEM

I just read an awful
poem about a yellow leaf
that the speaker mistakes
for a yellow butterfly. I'm
waiting to read the good
one in which a yellow
butterfly mistakes a yellow
leaf for a yellow butterfly
and tries to mate with it.

THE LAW OF ATTRACTION

It is said that all
the magnetic force
in the universe is not
equal to the force of
one magnet on the door
of your refrigerator, so
is this why I am more
attracted to my beer
than to the universe?

FALSE MODESTY

I would rather have
ten false starts
than one false ending.

A NOISELESS IMPATIENT SPIDER

I watched it cross the patio,
a noiseless (*Why the fuck*
hasn't anyone taken Whitman
to task over this nonsensical
adjective? Are there noisy
spiders? Really? Have you ever
heard a spider make any kind
of noise while spinning its web?
Or doing anything at all? Could
he have meant "noseless?")
impatient spider in a hurry in
its chosen direction from
sunshine into shadow, from
shadow into sunshine, to get
to the gap in the shed floor.

PROXIMITY

The orchard is next
to the cemetery.
This must be why
the honey crisp taste
so good. The crispy,
sweet dead.

WHEN THE DARK

When the dark
rain clouds moved
over, broad banks
of bright clouds
were left above
the rain clouds'
altitude to change
the whole day's
attitude left behind.

ENJOY YOURSELF

My mother's favorite song
was "Enjoy Yourself, It's Later
Than You Think." I think it
was the only song I ever
heard her sing. She sang it
in the kitchen while cooking
dinner. She sang it while
ironing sheets and shirts
and pillow cases. She sang it
in the basement of the building
doing the laundry. And when
she wasn't singing it, she
was humming it. She hummed
it while pushing my baby
brother in his stroller which
had been mine. She hummed it
in the car on our way up to
the Catskills in the summer.
"Enjoy yourself, it's later
than you think, enjoy yourself,
it's later than you think, later
than you think, later than you,
later than, later," and she was
right. It was later than we thought,
later than all four of us thought.

TELL ME AGAIN

Tell me again
what I was told

when I was young
what poetry is

supposed to do.
I am old.

I am old.
I have forgotten.

WE WERE TALKING ABOUT MOVIES

We were talking about movies.
Soon it got around to movies about
poets. *Beautiful Dreamers* is one
about Whitman. *Bright Star* about Keats.
A Quiet Passion about Dickinson.
Tm and Viv about Eliot and his wife.
Shakespeare in Love is about, well,
Shakespeare, but we agreed that he
doesn't count, and we agreed that poets
don't make good subjects for movies.
They're boring. Frost wouldn't be
good although he did threaten to kill
himself with a pistol at breakfast.
That would be a good scene. Stevens
wouldn't either despite the fact that
he was knocked down by Hemingway
at a cocktail party. Another good scene.
Bishop? Sure, she was a lesbian, but
not a good subject for a film. Boring.
Byron would be perfect for a movie.
He died in Greece fighting for their
independence. And that club foot of his.
A real challenge for Brad Pitt. Or Leo.
Bukowski did make a good subject.
An exception. An interesting movie
about a poet is *Paterson,* which is about
the hometown of William Carlos
Williams more than it's about him,
and about a bus driver in Paterson
who's a poet and whose name
is Paterson. Interesting but far
from the best. A really crazy movie
about a poet is *The Libertine* with

Johnny Depp as John Wilmot, Second
Earl of Rochester. Nothing if not
boring, especially the part where
his nose falls off from syphilis.
Speaking of Johnny Depp, wouldn't
he be an absolutely great Poe?
My favorite movie about a poet has
to be *If I Were King*, starring
Ronald Colman as Francois Villon.
And my favorite line (screenplay by
Preston Sturges) has to be this: "No
offense. Poetry is its own worst enemy."
Mais où sont les neiges d'antan?

THE CONCERT

It was boring.
It was Bach's Cantata #18.

It was boring.
"Just as the rain and snow fall from heaven"

It was boring as the rain.
It was boring as the snow.

It was boring as heaven.
There were other baroque pieces.

They were boring.
William Byrd was boring.

That other guy was boring.
I can't believe what I'm saying.

Bach was boring.
My beloved Bach was boring.

The closest thing in my book to divinity,
and he was boring.

Oh, god, he was so boring.
As boring as god.

RHETORICAL ANSWER

All things
end up

winding
down.

BEHIND ME THE SUNSET IS SPEAKING

Behind me the sunset is speaking.
"Listen carefully," it says.
"I am speaking from the heart."

Behind me a bird is speaking.
"Listen carefully," it says.
"I am speaking from the heart."

Behind me an insect is speaking.
"Listen carefully," it says.
"I am speaking from the heart."

Behind me a tree is speaking.
"Listen carefully," it says.
"I am speaking from the heart."

Behind me the breeze is speaking.
"Listen carefully," it says.
"I am speaking from the heart."

Behind me the lake is speaking.
"Listen carefully," it says.
"I am speaking from the heart."

"But that is the way you always speak,"
I say to the sunset, to the bird, to the insect,
to the tree, to the breeze, to the lake.

Behind me the sunset, the bird, the insect,
the tree, the breeze, the lake say, "Listen carefully.
We are laughing at you from the heart."

THE GIRL WHO ANSWERED THE PHONE

The girl who answered the phone
at the plumbing contractor said
I sounded like a happy person, and she
liked that. "Well," I said. "I'm happy
that you think I sound like a happy
person and are happy about it. But
I have to tell you something. I'm not
a happy person." "Really?" she said.
"How come?" "I'm a poet. Poets
aren't happy people," I said. "I don't
know any poets, so I couldn't say one
way or another. But you do sound happy.
You really do." She laughed. "You sound
like a happy poet." "That's an oxymoron,"
I said. "What's an ox-ee-mor-on?" She
stopped laughing. "An oxymoron is
a phrase with an adjective and a noun
that don't agree. They contradict one
another," I said. "*Jumbo shrimp* is a
good example." "Or a sad clown? Is that
an oxymoron?" "Yes," I said. "That's
a really good one." "Well," she said.
"I still think you sound like a happy
person, or poet or whatever you are.
And I still like it." "Me, too," I said.
Then I made the appointment for the
plumber just like any happy person would.

TO MY KNEES

How have you lasted so long?
Knees, you are seventy-three years
old, and you're still going strong.
You have never locked, never seized
up. I have no complaints about you.
You're not a pain in the neck. So
unlike my hips who live above you
and are awake all night making noise.
So unlike my shoulders who constantly
complain about the cold. Knees,
nothing seems to bother you. I'm lucky,
I suppose. Let me count my blessings –
one, two knees, one, two knees with wings.

TO MY ELBOWS

How many times, when
in a crowd, have I heard,
"They're so sharp!" about
you. Sharp as tacks, I'd say,
the way you get me through
to the front of things. And
let's not forget how I bend
you in bars to the perfect
angle of support, equilaterally
poised in three-point pose,
sometimes painfully acute,
but always right, always right.

THE SKY SHOULD BE SACROSANCT

The sky should be sacrosanct.
Only the birds should know it.
And the clouds when crossing over it.
And the rain and the snow when letting go of it.
The sky should be sacrosanct.
Only the sun should rule it by day.
Only the moon and stars should rule it by night.
No others must there be.
The engines there above me, they ought not be.
The sky should be free of them, the gross machines.
They should all, all be felled.
The sky should be free.
The sky should be sacrosanct.
May the Wright Brothers burn in hell.

I WENT INTO BANK SQUARE

I went into Bank Square
Coffee for coffee.
The television was on.
The president was on.
I gave the screen the finger.
I looked around. No one
was watching. Everyone
had their heads down.
Their heads were down.
Down, down were their
heads into their own
little screens. "This explains
everything," I said out loud.
No one looked up. No one
heard me, for all the heads
were down, down, down.
"Shit, this will explain
everything," I said to myself.
The coffee was good.
The best in town.

SOMEBODY CAME UP TO ME

Somebody came up to me
after the reading. "You write
too many poems about poetry,"
he said. "Really?" I said.
"Yeah," he said. "Too many
poems about writing poetry."
"Gee," I said. "I hadn't realized
that. Thanks for telling me.
But, you know, it's what I know
about more than anything else,
so it's natural that I write about
what I know about the most.
Is that bad?" "Well, it's not
bad exactly," he said. "So
what's the problem?" I asked.
"Well, you know, you should
write about other things," he
said. "Like what?" I said. "Well,"
he said. (He said "well" a lot.)
"Sunsets. Mountains. Birds.
Autumn leaves. Love." "Thanks
for the suggestion," I said. "But
I'll leave that to you."

from *The Time of Your Life*   2020

THE TIME OF YOUR LIFE

That was when there was time.
That lasted a long time.

Then life happened.
That lasted a short time.

Then life said, "It's your turn."
Time said, "Whatever, it's your life."

They were twins separated before birth.
They were together in passing.

They passed for each other.
They passed like ships in the night.

One winked.
The other waved.

I WAS OUT OF PLACE THERE

I was out of place there.
It was no place to be.

There was no place else to go.
There was no home-like place.

I hated hats.
I hated the fedora with the feather.

I hated the cab driver's cap.
I hated anything on my head.

I hated the skullcap.
I hated the hand.

I was the one who saw the butterfly.
I was the one who saw the omelet.

I was the one who did not see the blood.
I was the one who passed the test.

"We are the One, and they are the Zero," he said.
He was going fishing.

There was a marlin on the wall.
For a moment, I wished I had been one.

I envied his wild eye, and I envied his weapon.
One of us was out of place there.

PURPLE

Everyone looks good in it.
Everything looks wonderful in it.
The sky looks good in purple.
The purple marten looks wonderful in it.
The emperors and empresses,
regardless of their cruelty,
looked good, looked wonderful in purple.

I BOUGHT THEM

I bought them,
two big books,
fat with two lifetimes of poems,

not so much to read them,
which, over a long time, as is meant, I will do,
but just to look at,

their bigness,
heavy as loaves of grainy peasant bread,
and their pictures on the covers,

the two old Polish poets,
Milosz and Herbert,
their beautiful white hair,

their beautiful long white fingers,
their beautiful white cigarettes,
and the smoke like their own beautiful white ghosts.

THE MINK

It was the mink.
It was the mink with the glass bead eyes

and the satin lining that hung on the inside
of my mother's closet door.

It was the mink
with the glass bead eyes and the satin lining

that confused me so.
I was young.

I was confused.
It was how I did not know

why death should smell of fresh flowers,
why death could have such eyes

that confused me so.
I was a child.

I was confused.
It was for the rest of my life.

THE FIRST SEVEN STEPS OF THE BUDDHA-TO-BE

In the Qing dynasty bronze,
The First Seven Steps of the Buddha-To-Be,

the Buddha-To-Be has completed the seventh step.
He is standing motionless squarely on both feet.

He is pointing down with the index finger of his right hand.
He is pointing up with the index finger of his left hand.

He is saying, *I need go no farther. This is the way.
Here is the place between earth and heaven.*

So with his eighth step, the Buddha-To-Be
will forever stop counting steps.

MOVING IN

I am listening
to *The Flying Dutchman,*
that opera of redemption.
I cannot go

anywhere now
without leaving
myself in the snow.
Instead, I tack a poster

to the kitchen wall.
Instead, I hang a curtain
in the shower stall.
Instead, I put the sheets

on the bed.
Instead, I try to remember
what it was you said
before I left.

Instead, I put
the pillowcase
on the pillow.
Instead, I put my shoes

in place on the closet floor
and my underwear
in one dresser drawer,
sweaters in another,

pants on hangers.
Instead, I listen
to *The Flying Dutchman,*
that opera of redemption.

Instead, I put the saucepan
on the nail above
the greasy white
enamel stove.

Instead, I plug in
the electric typewriter
and write trash, write,
trash, hang flypaper.

Instead, I open
the cheap white wine.
Instead, I plug in
the electric typewriter

in a different outlet.
Instead, I hang a calendar.
Instead, I let out my Credo:
I believe in

this white of snow;
I believe in
this silver of moon;
I believe in

this music of redemption;
I believe in
this green of grass;
I believe in

this believing in less and less.
Here is the telephone,
this terrible instrument,
asleep in its cradle.

Here is the machine gun
of buttons, loaded weapon
of communication.
Who will be first

to call the other?
Who will be first
to pull the trigger?
Instead, I listen

to *The Flying Dutchman,*
that opera of redemption.
Instead, I write and trash.
Instead, I'm all moved in.

MASTURBATION

Sorry,
my mistake.

I got ahead
of myself.

THE MELANCHOLY OF ANATOMY

My hand hurts.
It's arthritis.

The pen hurts.
It's a poem.

VAN GOGH

painted 80 paintings
in the last 70 days
of his life. His last
is *Tree Roots*
painted the morning
of the day he died.
I want to write 80
poems in the last 70
days of my life.
The last will be
"Tree Roots," which
I will write the morning
of the day I die.
I want this because
van Gogh wanted
to be a poet,
because I wanted
to be a painter.

REASSURANCE

"Nothing's humming today," I said.
"Hey, don't complain," said Jim.
"Humming is what you do
when you've forgotten the words."

OVER THE CLOUDS

Over the clouds
the sun has no control.

They are in control,
the clouds, in their gray line,

not so much a line
as a mass, more than

massive enough to cover
the sun, to own, by force,

almost the sky whole.
Helpless, the sun

grins a gold grin
diminishing,

until it glows out,
goes gray as they

behind them,
finished off finishing.

THE NOWHERE

The nowhere
to be found

is not the same
nowhere

as the nowhere
to be seen.

THE MUSIC

The music is never irrelevant, never.
It is always the only way to travel, here or there.

Without music, the silence would be too much to bear.
Without music, the science would be too much to bear.

I want to die to music.
I want death to sing to blues guitar acoustic.

The physicists say the universe hums its own unaccompanied
        music.
If we had ears the size of galaxies, we could hear it.

When I die, my ears will be galaxies.
When I die, I will hear the universe hum its own unaccompanied
        music.

I will never forgive the gods for denying me a life in music.
Gods, with your ears of galaxies, do you hear?

I'd rather sing in Carnegie Hall once than write 1000 poems.
Death, do you hear me? (Sigh.)

I want you to set these words to blues guitar acoustic.
I tell you, if there is no music after death, I will die.

from *The Moon Is the Capital of the World*   2020

THE MOON IS THE CAPITAL OF THE WORLD

"What is the capital of the world?" my daughter asks.
"The moon is the capital of the world," I say.

It makes sense.
There is no city on earth that could be the capital of the world.

Not New York City. Not London. Not Paris. Not Beijing. Not
Tokyo.
Only the moon could be the capital of the world.

From there you could see the whole world.
That is what a capital of the world is for.

It is for seeing the whole world.
For seeing the world whole.

Warts and all.
Wars and all.

THE LADY OF THE NEWS

Every night I watch the lady of the news.
I do not like the news.
But I like her.
There is nothing to like about the news.
The news is all bad.
Every night the news is all bad.
But I like the lady of the news.
She does not have blonde hair.
She has black hair.
She does not have blue eyes.
She has black eyes.
She does not have fair skin.
She has dark skin.
She is not pretty that way that pretty is.
She is beautiful the way that beautiful is.
The news is neither pretty nor beautiful.
The news is ugly.
But I like to watch the lady of the news.
I like her voice.
Her voice is not pretty.
Her voice is beautiful.
Her voice delivers the ugly news beautifully.
If one must listen to bad news, this is the way to do it.

FOR THE PROVIDERS NOW A BIG BLESSING

For the doctor who fixed my sprained wrist,
now a big blessing,
for I could not have fixed my sprained wrist myself,

and for the dentist who replaced my broken molar,
now a big blessing,
for I could not have replaced my broken molar myself,

and for the dermatologist who removed my mole,
now a big blessing,
for I could not have removed my mole myself,

and for the nurse who bandaged the bad cut over my eye,
now a big blessing,
for I could not have bandaged the bad cut over my eye myself,

and for the surgeon who opened up my coronary artery,
now a big blessing,
for I could not have opened up my coronary artery myself,

and for the optometrist who gave me glasses to see with,
now a big blessing,
for I could not have given glasses to see with to myself.

I WANTED TO BE WHERE LITERAL IS LATERAL

I wanted to be where literal is lateral.
I wanted to be where simile is your umbrella.
I wanted to be where the only ladder is the ladder of her lad.
I wanted to be where all the towers are bell towers.
I wanted to be where worship has white sails.
I wanted to be where heaven is closed for repairs.
I wanted to be where poetry is the only currency.
I wanted to be where everything is sold for a song.
I wanted to be where gold is not.
I wanted to be where all I touch turns to silver.
I wanted to be where the moon is full every single night.
I wanted to be where I am alone but not for long.
I wanted to be where it is impossible to say, "I want."
I wanted to be where it is impossible to say, "I."
I wanted to be where literal is lateral.

RUMPELSTILTSKIN

So let the psychologists point fingers.
So let the folklorists remark.
I had a childhood.
It was no worse than any.
I had a mother.
She was no worse than any.
I had a father.
He was no worse than any.
I was an only child.
So were thousands and thousands.
She thought she could cheat me because I am ugly.
The pretty do not know what love is.
The beautiful do not know what suffering is.
I know a man, a poet.
He is a good friend of mine.
We are blood brothers.
He's as "handsome as hell."
That's a direct quote.
A lady said that.
It means nothing to him.
"Vanitas vanitatum," he says.
His suffering is greater than mine.
The tale is my tale.
My name is on it.

READING

As I crossed
the stage to
the lectern,
I wasn't sure
how my poems
would come across.

THE BAY

Do you know the bay?
Do you know the bay at sunrise?

Do you know the bay at sunset?
Do you know the bay at midnight?

Do you know the bay when it is wearing the stars on its back?
Do you know the bay when it is hiding in the fog?

Do you know the bay when it is baying at the moon?
Do you know the bridge?

Do you know the bridge over the bay?
Do you ever wish you were on the other side?

Do you ever wish there were no other side?
Do you ever dream of bay seahorses?

Do you know the island of prisoners in the bay?
Do you ever want to know what crimes they committed?

Do you ever want the same punishment for your own crimes?
Do you know that pigeon that glided by by the bay?

Do you think it was an angel?
Do you think it was the wrong city for an angel to glide by?

Do you think it was a saint?
Do you think it was Saint Francis of Assisi?

Do you ever wonder if Saint Francis of Assisi ever saw a gull?
Do you ever wonder if Assisi is on a bay?

Do you know Assisi is in central Italy, hence not on a bay?
Do you ever wonder what it is to be a flag fluttering over the bay?

Do you ever want to cruise the world as if it were a bay?
Do you ever want to cruise through life as if it were a bay?

Do you ever want to know how it feels to be land sick?
Do you ever want to shout, "Stop thief!"

Do you ever want to shout, "She has stolen my heart!"
Do you ever want to shout, "She has taken my heart back to San
        Jose!"

Do you know the bay by heart?
Do you know how to keep your heart at bay?

MARY MURPHY

Mary Murphy, Mary Murphy, Mary Murphy,
did I make you up?
Did I dream you came to the door that day?
Did I dream your wore a sheer white slip on the top floor?
Mary Murphy, Mary Murphy, Mary Murphy,
did I make you up when I was six that day?
Did I dream my mother sent me to your door on the top floor?
Did I dream you opened the door in your sheer white slip?
Did I dream you exclaimed, "O, Joel, wait!" and closed the door?
Did I dream you came back to give me the sugar she asked for?
Did I dream you had red hair, red hair, red hair?
Did I make up that heaven on the top floor of 247?
Did I dream you laughed, you laughed, you laughed at me?
Mary Murphy, Mary Murphy, Mary Murphy,
I was six and could not make you up.
I was six and could not make up your red hair.
I was six and could not make up your sheer white slip.
I was six and a Jew and could not make up a Catholic like you.
I was six and a Jew and could not make up an Irish colleen like you.
Mary Murphy, Mary Murphy, Mary Murphy,
I was six and a Jew and could not make up an angel like you.
I was six and a Jew and could not make up the heaven of
        you on the top floor.
I was six and I could not make up how you laughed at me.
Mary Murphy, Mary Murphy, Mary Murphy.

GUEST OF THE SKY

When you fly, you are the guest of the sky.
When you fly, you say goodbye to gravity.
When you fly, you are attentive to the flight attendant.
When you fly, you explain why you are standing in the galley.
When you fly, you tell her you have sciatica.
When you fly, you are on your best behavior.
When you fly, you wear your Sunday civility.
When you fly, you attend to her talk of Ventura.
When you fly, you attend to her talk of surfing.
When you fly, you attend to her talk of her son in Vienna.
When you fly, you get up from your seat to leave later.
You do not say, "Goodbye."
You look her in the sky blue eye and say, "Take care of yourself."

THE ROOF

The roof is the blessing of the house.
The roof keeps its hands on the walls.
Only the roof knows the sky and what comes from the sky.
The roof knows the birds by heart.
The roof knows the clouds inside out.
The windows think they know the sky,
but they are mistaken.
Because no one visits it,
the roof is the loneliest part of the house.
Because no one visits it,
the roof is the wisest part of the house.

MY AUDIENCE

"Who is your audience?"
someone asked. That was
easy. It's the old peasant
woman in the Chinese village
who cannot read or write
to whom I imagine I read
my poems, and if she does
not understand every word,
I rewrite them until she does.
She is my audience.

THE TRACKS

The tracks are easy to keep track of.
The tracks are not going anywhere.
The tracks head out of the woods from the north.
The tracks head into the woods to the south.
The tracks are in the clear at the crossing where they are
        double-crossed.
The tracks are parallel lines that never meet.
The tracks are Euclid's children.
The tracks make for fellow Euclideans.
The tracks have at least two followers who are poets.
The tracks are the tracks of the train.
The tracks of an animal tell where it has been.
The tracks of a train tell where it will be.
The train does not need to train the tracks.
The train simply trains the tracks.
The train can switch its tracks with the motion of a hand.
The train wears a star on its face.
The star twinkles in the daylight and in the dark of night.
The train hauls the moon behind it.
The train comes and becomes the tracks.
Then the tracks become the train.
When the train comes, the sound of sex is in the air.
The train comes in the middle of the night bound south.
It awakens me with its loud boundless sound of sex from its
        mouth.

from *Piano Music*   2020

PIANO MUSIC

The piano is tired of waiting.
The piano closes up shop.
The piano, a three-legged black stallion, wants to gallop away.
The piano's forte is silence.
The piano says, "Hands off."
The piano keeps its thoughts to itself.
The piano possesses the keys to the kingdom.
The piano knows black plus white does not equal gray.
The piano knows black plus white equals blue.
(Nota bene: The piano knows its way.)
The piano says, "Follow me."
The piano says, "I'm in your hands."
The piano is depressed when it is not depressed.
The piano tunes out cacophony.
The piano spits out phony.
The piano doesn't stand on formality although formal.
The piano hugs its little sister harp.
The piano makes a grand entrance.
The piano always speaks true although not always uprightly.
The piano is touched by your sincerity.
The piano touches you with 88 fingers.
The piano touches you.

SO I GOT LOST

So I went inside.
So I sat at the table by the window.

So I sat in the chair facing the door.
So the server came over to serve me.

So I said water.
So the server came with the water.

So I said the moon.
So the server said the full moon or the half moon.

So I said the full moon.
So the server said with the clouds or with the stars.

So I said with the stars.
So the server said with which wine.

So I said with which wine.
So the server said with the white.

So I said with the white.
So the server came with the full moon, the stars and the white
      wine.

So I had the full moon, the stars, and the white wine.
So I went outside.

So in the sky was no moon.
So in the sky were no stars.

So in the sky were only clouds.
So it was dark.

So I got lost.
So I went inside.

THE BIBLE IN THE DRAWER IN THE ROOM OF THE HOTEL

It was never opened.
I was the first to open it.
It felt good.
It felt bad.
I did not open it to read it.
I read it once.
I will never read it again.
I opened it to hear it crack.
The same as the new textbooks in school.
I liked to hear them crack.
It cracked the crack of the shell of a nut.
It cracked the crack of a cockroach stepped upon.
It cracked the crack of an ice cube in a glass of whiskey.
It cracked the crack of a wishbone.
It felt good.
It felt bad.

NOW THAT

Now that that
ash tree is cut
down and out
of the way,
the new light
can light the way
for new trees to
come in that way.

DISNEY

He hated Jews.
I hated Mickey Mouse.
We were even.

AND THEN IN THE ARMS OF THE GALAXY WITH THE SPIRAL ARMS

And then I shall spiral out of control.
And then I shall sing the sad cradle song.

And then I shall spiral out of control.
And then I shall sing the sad lullaby.

And then I shall spiral out of control.
And then I shall sing the sad love song.

And then I shall spiral out of control.
And then I shall sing the sad funeral dirge.

And then I shall spiral out of control.
And then I shall spiral in the arms of the galaxy with the
    spiral arms.

WHEN THE CLOCK BROKE

When the clock broke, time died.
So I brought time to the time repair shop.
The time repairman examined time.
"I can repair your time," he said.
"How much will it cost?" I said.
He told me how much.
"How much is a new time?" I said.
He told me how much.
"I can repair this time," he said.
"It will be as good as new."
"Okay," I said. "Go ahead and fix
my old time if it will be as good as new."
"But it only comes with a one-year warranty," he said.
"But you said it will be as good as new," I said.
"That's right," he said.
"That's what we time repairmen call a paradox."

ORCHARDS

"Wow, what big peaches," I said.
"Are they bigger than last year?"
"They are," the owner said. "But
there are fewer than last year."
"How come?" I said. "The weather,"
she said. "A lot of rain. More than
normal. And not enough sunny days
to dry things out a little. Less than
normal sun." "So it's a metaphor,"
I said. "How's that?" she said. "You
know," I said. "A short but gloriously
full life or a long but average life."
"I'd rather have a bigger harvest of
smaller peaches," she said. "My living
depends on it." " I'm the opposite,"
I said. "I'd rather have a handful
of glorious poems than a truckload
of average ones. My immortality
depends on it." "That's the difference
between poems and peaches, I suppose,"
she said. "By the way, I enjoyed your
new book. The peaches are free."

A FAIRY TALE

Once upon a time, Once-Upon-A-Time wanted to be an ending and not a beginning. It was tired of being a beginning all the time. It envied Happily-Ever-After who was never tired of being the happy ending all the time. So Once-Upon-A-Time went to the palace to see The-King. "What do you want?" asked The-King. "I am tired of being the beginning all the time," said Once-Upon-A-Time. "I want to be the happy ending like Happily-Ever-After." "Makes no difference to me who the beginning is or who the ending is," said The-King. "Just as long as I'm in the middle of it all and my daughter The-Princess is happy." "So I can be the ending?" said Once-Upon-A-Time. "Sure, why not?" said The-King. "But what would you have me do with Happily-Ever-After?" "Well, he can take my place at the beginning," said Once-Upon-A-Time. "I see," said The-King. "Okay, let's give it a try." The-King sent for Happily-Ever-After. "Listen," said The-King. "I have decided that you, Happily-Ever-After, trade places with Once-Upon-A-Time. Understood?" "Well, no," said Happily-Ever-After. "I don't understand, but you're The-King, so I'll give it a try." And give it a try they did. One try after another. One fairy tale after another. But try as they might, it just didn't work. Everybody was confused and laughed at them and blamed The-King and The-Princess was not happy. Moral of the story: Never make The-Princess cry. Second Moral of the story: Never blame The-King.

MAIN STREET

It's where you go to look in windows.
It's where you go to read the news.
It's where you go to see the widows.
It's where you go to hear the blues.

It's where to go to buy the duct tape.
It's where to go to drink the beer.
It's where to go to eat a crepe.
It's where you go to sniff and sneer.

It's where you go to get the coffees.
It's where you go to get a snip.
It's where you go to see divorcees.
It's where you go to get a grip.

It's there, there, all there is is there.
It's where you go to be somewhere.

from *A Guide of the Perplexed*   2020

THE GUIDE FOR THE PERPLEXED

When I was nineteen or twenty,
I started to read
The Guide for the Perplexed
by Moses Maimonides.
I was nineteen or twenty.
I was perplexed.
I needed a guide.
I read a few pages
by the great Jewish sage.
Perhaps I read a chapter.
I don't remember.
But I soon realized I needed
a guide to the guide.
I have never gone back to read
what was next
in *The Guide for the Perplexed*
by Moses Maimonides.
It's not my fault.
He should have illustrated the text
with pictures of flowers.
Roses and tulips and daisies.
Or just a little sex.

AMERICA

The notebook I am writing in was made in China
The pen I am writing with was made in China.
The chair I am sitting on was made in China.
The desk I am sitting at was made in China.
The frames of the glasses I am seeing with were made in China.
The glass I am drinking from was made in China.
But the bourbon I am drinking was made in America.
And the poem I am writing was made in America.
And that's enough America for me.

WHEN THE WIND STOPS

When the wind stops,
the leaves stop falling
while those already
fallen stop skittering
along the ground and
pause before the cul-de-
sacs of wall and fence
or fence and shed or shed
and steps or steps and wall.

WHEN I ASKED

When I asked,
he didn't know
the first thing
about it. This
is very bad, for
one thing is all
there ever is to
know about it.

THE DELIVERY

The UPS driver delivered
a boxful of my new book.
I gave him one. "You're
a writer?" he said. "No,"
I said. "I'm a poet." "Oh,
is there a difference?" he
said. "Yes, writers write to
be understood. Poets write
to be remembered," I said.
"Well, I'll remember you,"
he said. "Good," I said.
"Also it couldn't hurt
to understand what you
remember." "Got it," he said.

NOW THAT IT'S THREE O'CLOCK

Now that it's three o'clock,
I wish this were a civilized country.

Now that it's three o'clock,
I wish this were Moorish Spain,

where the Christians, Muslims and Jews
lived together in peace and harmony.

Now that it's three o'clock,
I wish this were a civilized country

where the Christians, the Muslims and the Jews drank wine,
wrote poems and talked philosophy far into the night.

Now that it's three o'clock,
I wish this were a civilized country.

MY JAPANESE DEATH POEM

When I die, bury me
with an acorn
in my mouth.
Then at least one
of us might become
the mighty oak tree
that both our mothers
wanted done.

I WALK THE RAILROAD TRACKS

I walk the railroad tracks
with you as my mind's companion,

Galway Kinnell, your fellow Euclidean.
The tracks are straight here.

They point straight to where they vanish through the trees.
You were eighty-seven. I am seventy-three.

The prostate is enlarged, the arthritis worsening.
I'm on the way, all right.

Now, for the first time in my life, I see it, Galway.
I see the point in vanishing completely out of sight.

BREAKFAST

I eat oatmeal for breakfast.
Sometimes I eat oat bran.
Just for the sake of a little variety.
Unlike Kinnell, I do not invite John Keats to eat breakfast with
    me.
Did John Keats even eat breakfast?
He was tubercular.
So he didn't eat much at all.
His favorite food was roast beef sandwiches.
Walter Scott said that cold roast beef was the ideal breakfast
    dish.
Keats probably knew that.
So, no, I would not think Keats ate oatmeal.
It doesn't matter.
I've always preferred Coleridge over Keats, anyway.
And Blake over both.
I drink coffee standing at the kitchen window.
I once wondered why oatmeal is one word while oat bran is two
    words.
I researched it, but couldn't find out.
I look at the birds eat breakfast at the feeders.
I do not invite John Keats.
I eat breakfast alone.
The way breakfast should be eaten.
The way Blake ate breakfast while watching the angels through
    his window.

THERE IS A BOOK THAT REFUSES TO BE WRITTEN

There is a book that refuses to be written.
There is a book with a spine made of steel.
There is a book whose pages are of silver.
There is a book that can be read only in moonlight.
There is a book that can be read only by near-sighted eyes.
There is a book that would rather die than be written.
There is a book too proud to be read.
There is a book that cannot keep a secret.
There is a book that wants to be a book that no one has read.
There is a book that wants its name on everyone's lips.
There is a book that wants to be sworn on.
There is a book that wants young ladies to swoon over.
There is a book that wants to be held in your hands.
There is a book that wants to be blank.
There is a book that says, "Keep your hands off me."
There is a book that wants to stare without blinking.
There is a book. There is a book. There is a book.

ONCE I WANTED A MIND

Once I wanted a mind
that could know
what the world was thinking.

Once I wanted eyes
that could see
right through to the very heart of things.

Once I wanted ears
that could hear
the secrets the stars whisper to one another.

Once I wanted feet
that could carry me
around the earth as swiftly as light.

Once I wanted a voice
that could sing
my song so loud the moon would hear.

Once I wanted a heart
so welcoming,
so giving, it would love all equally.

That was once.
Now my mind, my eyes, my ears, my feet,
my voice, my heart have better things to do.

SOMEDAY

Someday
the last poet

in the world
will write

the world's
last poem.

This too
will be

anonymous.
This too

will be in a
dead language.

This too
will be

a hymn
to the sun.

from *Years Later*   2021

I SAW ALL OF THEM

I saw all of them.
I saw all of them going off.
I saw all of them going on the highways.
I saw all of them lying low, not wanting to be seen.
I heard all of them.
I heard all of them lying.
I heard all of them telling the truth when it suited them.
I saw all of them in their suits of silver and gold.
I saw all of them in their pantsuits of platinum.
I saw all of them in their sweaters of species endangered.
I saw all of them in their scarves of scarcity.
I saw all of them in their shoes of extinction.
I heard all of them smirk into their wrists.
I heard all of them cackle into the airy ears of nowhere.
I heard all of them swear.
I saw all of them walk through the door held open by the doormen.
I heard the doormen curse in their own language so no one could
        hear.
I saw their teeth flash like neon at night.
I saw their eyes shine and glow, one of silver, one of gold.
I heard their lips suck the milk of diamonds.
I heard the soft hum of the handshake.
I heard the swift whish of whisky.
I heard the tight tinkle of ice.
I saw the deal of the dead.
I saw all of them head for the exits.
I heard all of the earth exhale in all its languages.
I saw all of the earth head for the exit.

O, GIVE US THE ABERRANTS!

And we shall nail one to our doors.
And we shall wear one around our necks.
And we shall bronze one like our baby shoes.
And we shall frame one within silver.
And we shall wrap one in linen.
And we shall emblazon one upon our banners.
And we shall emboss one upon our shields.
And we shall incise one into the steel of our swords.
And we shall weave one into the clothes of our cause.
And we shall brand one upon the stainless flesh of our foreheads.

I AM WAITING FOR HEAVEN TO STOP FALLING

O, heaven is falling!
Where will the angels go?
Where will the angels live?

They cannot live here.
They cannot live on earth.
They will not know how to live here with us.

O, heaven is falling down!
Where will the angels go?
Where will the angels live?

They will not be welcome here.
We will not welcome them here.
We will build a roof against them.

O, heaven is falling!
O, the rest of the angels are falling!
Let us build a roof over our heads to keep off the angels!

It is of the angels I am thinking.
It is of the angels, not of us.
It is of the angels.

MORRIS KARP

Morris Karp was born in Russia.
Morris Karp was the father of my mother.
Morris Karp came to America in 1910.

Morris Karp spoke only Russian
Morris Karp learned English in America.
Morris Karp got a job operating a sewing machine in America.

Morris Karp made pockets for businessmen's jackets in America.
Morris Karp made pockets for businessmen's coats in America.
Morris Karp knew injustice in America.

Morris Karp did not know the word *injustice*.
Morris Karp was active in the union of garment workers.
Morris Karp fought for a 40-hour week.

Morris Karp fought for decent conditions of work.
Morris Karp fought for a living wage.
Morris Karp was beaten by a police officer on the street.

Morris Karp showed me the scar he got in America.
Morris Karp showed me the perfect pockets he made in America.
Morris Karp told me something.

Morris Karp told me how he learned the difference between
      tear and *tear.*
Morris Karp said, *A tear is a tear in your eye.*
Morris Karp said, *A tear is a tear in your pocket.*

THERE SHOULD HAVE BEEN ANOTHER MYTH

A myth is missing.
There never were enough.
There has always been a space.
It has always been a chasm too wide to cross.
There has always been a burning question.
It has always burned the tongue.
There has always been the gaping gap between the hills.
It has always been impossible for the moon to fill.
A myth is missing.
It should have been.
It should have been meant to explain the future.
It should have been meant to explain the origin of failure.
It should have been meant to explain how fire begat desire.
A myth is missing.
There should have been one more.
There should have been one more behind the temple door.
Certainly a myth is missing.

THERE ARE TWO FLAGS THERE

There are two flags there.
One flag has stripes of red and white.
It has white stars upon a field of blue.
The other flag has a snake chopped up in pieces.
The chopped up snake is upon a field of yellow.
The yellow is a garish yellow.
The chopped up snake has a rattle on its tail.
There is a motto.
The motto reads, *Don't tread on me.*
The first flag has no motto.
Perhaps it should have had a motto.
Perhaps it should have been, *Forgive me.*

THE WORD WORE WHITE

There was a wedding.
It was a private wedding.
No one was invited.
It was the wedding of the word.
The word was marrying the old man.
It was the word's first marriage.
It was the old man's second marriage.
The word was not a virgin.
The word slept with thousands of old men.
The old man was not a virgin but felt like one.
The word wore white.
The old man wore black.
The old man believed he was at a funeral.
It was a reasonable belief.

OFFICE HOUR

I don't understand this poem,
Mr. S., she said. Which one?
I said. "The King of Ice Cream"
by Steven Wallace, she said.
Okay, I said. Let's talk about
"The Emperor of Ice Cream"
by Wallace Stevens, I said.
Know what? I said. What?
she said. I don't understand
it either, I said. You don't?
she said. Nope, I said. But
you're the teacher, she said.
That's right, I said. I'm
the teacher, so now I'll
teach you something. Think
of the poem as a conversation
starter. A conversation starter?
Yes, Something that starts
a conversation. What you and I
are doing right now. You mean
having a conversation? That's
right. But we're having half
of the conversation. Go home
and have the other half of
the conversation with the poem.
Then come back, and we'll
continue our conversation.
Okay, she said. She didn't.

EMPHASIS IS ALL

Life is not
like that.

Life is like
that.

SAINT STONE

Once a man
named Stone
had the plan
of his very own
to become a saint
by simply painting
his face and hands
with silver paint.
So he spent his fortune
on silver paint
and painted his face
and hands, and now
he is known
as Saint Stone
all over the place.

YEARS LATER

Years later, the words were faded. The ink, once purple-black, was the ghost of brown. It was like the beech leaves scattered over the myrtle. The paper, once the white of cream, was the yellow-white of weathered paint, an old sailboat's hull. But beneath it, the photograph of the three of us was unchanged. It was still black and white. I was still stupidly self-conscious. You were still beautiful. He was still in front and between us, still slightly leaning into you. His face was still that haiku of eyes and mouth. Months later, spring came. Beneath the forsythia, the crocus appeared, head first. Some were purple. Some were yellow. Some were white. The rain was not icy anymore. The nebulous desires came into focus. The heart opened. It put forth its spike of fire. It burned purple. It burned yellow. It burned white. Weeks later, I remembered it. There was nothing more to learn by heart. There was nothing more to discover there. Two pleasures had to be enough, and they were enough. One pleasure had to be enough, and it was enough. Days later, the cloud shaped like a man in recline who has dreamed he has dreamed the three perfect dreams of the world, moved off on the wind. It revealed the moon. The moon was silent. The moon was silver. The moon was cold. The moon was the three perfect dreams of the world. Moments later, all was gone. The golden-yellow of the sun, the white of the clouds, the clear and endless blue of the sky were gone. All that was reflected in the window of the train was in the eyes and the mouth. The eyes blinked. The mouth opened. It was years later.

MY LAST POEM

It will be about spring.
I will write it in the dead of winter.

It will be dark pink in the middle.
It will be the exact color of magnolia blossoms.

Around its edges, it will be the precise white of wild cherry.
Or it will be the other way around.

This I will decide at the last moment.
A warm breeze will blow gently between the blank spaces.

It will be lifted up to be read.
Then the words will fall, slantwise, from the page into the palm
        of my hand.

There they will leave a fragrance at once familiar and strange.
No amount of water, nor any of prose, will ever wash it away.

from *The Dust* 2021

THE DUST

Let the dust settle.
Let it settle where it pleases.
Let the dust find its places.
Let the dust found its settlement mounds.
Let the dust settle the matter.
Let it be a matter of life and death.
It will be a matter of life and death anyway.
Let it be pretended that you let it.
Pretend that you let yourself in.
It does no harm.
Pretend that you let yourself out.
It does no harm.
The dust does not discriminate.
The dust shows no favoritism.
It doesn't matter to the dust.
The dust gathers in the corner.
The dust gathers under the desk.
The dust insinuates in my socks.
This mote is from the moon.
This mote is from the stars.
What matters most is what most matters.
A mote upon a mote is a totem.
The ancestors of the dust are the moon and the stars.
The descendants of the dust are just us.

GOLDEN

There is a golden cover on the book.
There is a golden book because it has a golden cover.
There is a golden poet on the cover.
There is a golden star in the sky.
There is golden light all over everything.
The golden poet writes poems in golden ink.
How much would a poem be worth if a poem were worth its
      weight in gold?
That is the golden question of the day.
There is a golden look on his face.
I am talking about the poet on the golden cover.
There is a golden voice in the poems.
I am talking about the golden poet's golden poems.
I am talking about gold.
It is difficult to talk about gold when you mean golden and not gold.
It is the color golden that I am talking about.
It is the color golden that has no worth.
It is the color golden that glisters.
It is the Golden Apple of the Sun.
It is the prize of no worth.
It is the prize all precious.
It is the only prize worth prizing.
Gold, gold, golden gold.
What is the price of gold that is priceless?
That is the second golden question of the day.
He was born with a golden tongue in his mouth.
He was born with a golden stake in his heart.
"Silence is golden," they say.
"Gold is silent," says he.

A SHOTGUN

I asked to see a shotgun. Which is the best?
I asked. This one, she said. She handed me
a 12 gauge, 6 shot, pump action shotgun.
It was heavy. I almost dropped it. She smirked.
I aimed at the wall. I pumped the pump.
I pulled the trigger. I pumped and pulled.
Pumped and pulled. Pumped and pulled. Six
times I pumped and pulled. I was pretending
12 gauge shotgun shells were blasting the wall.
I was starting to enjoy it. I was finding a rhythm.
It felt like writing a poem. It felt like writing
a 12 gauge 6 shot pump action poem. Give it
here, she said. I handed her the gun. Thanks,
I said, What do you want this for? she asked.
I don't know, I said. Hunting? she asked. No,
I said. I don't hunt. For home defense then?
she asked. Yes, I said. I want it for home defense.
I understand, she said. Because it's a different
world. No, I said. Because it isn't. I didn't get
it. I'll take my chances with the world unarmed.

TODAY I WORE A T-SHIRT

Today I wore a t-shirt
with the face of a wolf.
If reincarnation is true,
then I would want to come
back as a wolf. A gray
wolf, or a red wolf, or
any wolf on the list of
endangered species. If
I returned in my next life
as a wolf on the edge of
extinction, I could do such
things, I could do such
things, I tell you, I could
do such wonderfully awful
things I cannot tell you.

DEAF CHILD AREA

I slow down and look
around whenever I drive
by the house, not ever
knowing what I expect
to see exactly, except
a child at the window
waving at me, maybe.
I really would like to
see that one day. Just
once. I really would love
to wave back. Just once.

IN CASE

In case you
have no soul,
it is your heart
that you must sell
to the devil.

TO BEN WHO LIKED MY POEM, "ENOUGH IS ENOUGH"

Ben, you are right.
That is a good poem.
Thanks for saying so.
I hope it encourages
you to write poetry
yourself. One word of
advice, though. Don't
use "Fuck this!" in
every poem. It will spoil
the effect. Use it sparingly.
Once is enough. And
the same goes for
"son-of-a-bitch."

THE DEVIL'S VILLANELLE

I hear you want to write a villanelle.
Listen up. Look right here. I'll show you how.
Just follow this form through. (Or go to hell.)

Sit down. Turn on the lamp. Get comfortable.
Get paper out. And pen. All ready? Wow!
Okay. Let's write the perfect villanelle.

You're lacking confidence, I see. Well, well.
My method's guaranteed. Sure fire. Just vow
to follow this form through. (Or go to hell.)

No strings attached. I trade. I never sell.
I'm here to help. No need to start a row.
Scratch here to write the perfect villanelle.

Your soul? Zero. Nada. Zilch. Can't you tell?
Quick. Beads of sweat are breaking on your brow.
Quick. Follow this form through. (Or go to hell.)

Where ya going? Giving up so soon? Swell!@#%&*
Hey, you called me, you know. Don't have a cow!
Then don't. Don't write the perfect villanelle.
Just follow this fork, you, and come to hell.

SOUL

The valley has a soul.
The valley's soul is the river.

But the river, because it is a soul, does not have one.
So which do you wish to be?

Do you wish to have a soul or to be a soul?
Do you wish to be the valley or the river?

Or do you wish to be the mountain above the valley,
above the river, the very soul of above it all?

REQUEST

When the man in the next
room died,
his daughter gave
his flowers to the nurses,
so Emily, my daughter,
listen to me, when I am the man
in the next room,
give my flowers to the homeliest nurse only.

CROSSING THE BAR

What's on tap? I asked the barmaid.
The barmaid gave me the beer menu.
I see you don't have the one I want.
What's that? she asked. Lethe, I said.
I never heard of Lethe, she said,
pronouncing it *leth*. It's Lethe, I said.
It's the name of a river in hell.
Oh, she said. Isn't that the Styx?
she said, pronouncing it *stikes*. That's
a different river, I said. The Styx is
the one you cross to get to hell,
the underworld. The Lethe is the one
you drink from once you're there
to wash away all your memories, I said.
You forget everything about the upper
world. Oh, she said. I guess that means
we do have it on tap. All the beers do
that, make you forget, don't they?
she said. Like Lethe IPA, Lethe amber
ale, Lethe stout, Lethe red, Lethe wheat?
She was pronouncing it right. Yes, I said.
You're absolutely right. I'll have a Lethe
stout. She wasn't as dumb blonde as she looked.

I WAS LOOKING FOR THE IMPORTANT ONE

I was looking for the important one.
I looked in the drawers.
I looked in the closets.
I looked in the pantry.
I looked under the kitchen sink.
I looked under the bathroom sink.
I looked under the other bathroom sink.
I looked in the attic.
I looked in the basement.
I looked in the garage.
I looked on the book shelves.
I looked in my pockets.
I looked in the mirror.
I looked everywhere for the important one.
I found it finally.
It was in the wastepaper basket.
It was under all the other important ones.

PRESENT

To the future
I leave
the past I left.

J.R. Solonche has published poetry in more than 400 magazines, journals, and anthologies since the early 70s. He is the author of *Beautiful Day* (Deerbrook Editions), *Won't Be Long* (Deerbrook Editions), *Heart's Content* (Five Oaks Press), *Invisible* (nominated for the Pulitzer Prize by Five Oaks Press), *The Black Birch* (Kelsay Books), *I, Emily Dickinson & Other Found Poems* (Deerbrook Editions), *In Short Order* (Kelsay Books), *Tomorrow, Today and Yesterday* (Deerbrook Editions), *True Enough* (Dos Madres Press), *The Jewish Dancing Master* (Ravenna Press), *If You Should See Me Walking on the Road* (Kelsay Books), *In a Public Place* (Dos Madres Press), *To Say the Least* (Dos Madres Press), *The Time of Your Life* (Adelaide Books), *The Porch Poems* (Deerbrook Editions , 2020 Shelf Unbound Notable Indie Book), *Enjoy Yourself* (Serving House Books), *Piano Music* (nominated for the Pulitzer Prize by Serving House Books), *For All I Know* (Kelsay Books), *A Guide of the Perplexed* (Serving House Books), *The Moon Is the Capital of the World* (Word Tech Communications), *Years Later* (Adelaide Books), *The Dust* (Dos Madres Press), and coauthor with his wife, Joan I Siegel, of *Peach Girl: Poems for a Chinese Daughter* (Grayson Books). He lives in the Hudson Valley.

Printed in the USA
CPSIA information can be obtained
at www.ICGtesting.com
LVHW092256201123
764200LV00005B/2